Initiation Into Reality

First published by O-Books, 2011
O-Books is an imprint of John Hunt Publishing Ltd., Laurel House, Station Approach,
Alresford, Hants, SO24 9JH, UK
office1@o-books.net
www.o-books.com

For distributor details and how to order please visit the 'Ordering' section on our website.

ISBN: 978-1-84694-523-6

A CIP catalogue record for this book is available from the British Library.

Design: David Kirby
Cover design: Design Deluxe

Cover picture: James Christie
Hands of the Lemurian woman giving a piece of gold: Bintou Balde

Printed and bound by CPI Group (UK) Ltd, Croydon, CR0 4YY
Printed in the USA by Offset Paperback Mfrs, Inc

We operate a distinctive and ethical publishing philosophy in all
areas of our business, from our global network of authors to
production and worldwide distribution.

Initiation Into Reality

Truth Revealed Again

Hans Meijer

BOOKS

Winchester, UK
Washington, USA

Contents

Preface

Dedication

*To all the people who want to
contribute to a better world*

Preface

All world religions have a mystical tradition, the deeper content of which usually stays hidden. It is referred to as 'Secret knowledge'. However, it is not to deny this knowledge to people that it is 'secret'. Rather, it remains hidden because it is almost impossible to express its essence in words. For this reason, mystics mostly use symbols or metaphors when they want to reveal the hidden gold to spiritual seekers.

The mystical knowledge is, in fact, the heart of each religion. Where religion is not correctly understood (and consequently people lose interest), most likely it's because the mystical heartbeat is no longer perceived. When this is the case, people lose touch with their source and therefore lose insight into the meaning of existence.

To the extent that the great world religions have lost their mystical heart, we can say: this book surpasses religion. When we listen to the mystical heartbeat of each religion we say:
here all religions come together.

How religions come together in this book is best shown by formulating the essence of the book as:

The Absolute has become you,
Your Self is the Absolute.
So, uncover the Absolute!

Initiation into Reality aims to open you to the truth of this statement, and to guide you toward your own experience of the Absolute. The Absolute is Reality.

The realization of the Absolute, Reality, changes your life completely. Some characteristics of the Absolute given in these pages are: the timeless, the eternal, the imperishable, the good, perfect peace, pure love, God… So, it is no wonder that the insight into that Absolute gives your life a totally different meaning. A completely new, spiritual dimension is added.

In this book, it is also stated that the cause of all the misery in the world is the fact that man is not conscious of his relationship with the Absolute. Because of this, we just live from our ego without contact with the 'source': the roots of our existence. Although we need this contact, this reunification with our source, we are almost never aware of this need.

In essence, man is a religious, mystical being. Our primal spiritual need for reunification with our source, however, remains hidden because of another fundamental need: namely, our sexual need. This we know, but we do not understand it properly.

It is, in fact, our primal spiritual need for reunification, which makes us look for what we think will make us happy. In a positive way, this will usually lead us to seek security in a perfect relationship, a family or a career. In a negative way, this can lead to the glorifying of the ego, the longing for power and the satisfaction of desires.

Mankind's tragedy is that real mystic wisdom, as I will try to explain, is apparently no longer available. Why not? Did we all lose this knowledge? Has this knowledge not been revealed before? Of course it has. This knowledge dates back thousands and thousands of years, but its meaning is no longer understood. Because of our ignorance of the spiritual Reality of existence, and the fact that as a result we live separated from the mystical source of life, it is with the mind that we vainly try to solve our human problems.

When the primal need for reunification with the source of our existence cannot be fulfilled in a satisfying way, we become lonely, depressed, or sad. Another way of responding to our lack of 'contact' with our primal source is the 'inflation' of our ego. All kinds of human disasters can be created this way. This is the origin of crime, war, exploitation, discrimination, and all other negative things.

We all know that in politics (national as well as international), one is seriously looking for ways to manage the constantly growing problems of the world. Where is one looking for solutions? Everywhere but where these solutions will really be found. The only real solution for all human issues is found when humanity opens to wisdom. Mankind without wisdom will, by losing the understanding of the meaning of life, annihilate itself.

Living from wisdom, from insight into Reality, leads to taking responsibility, to the preservation of life. But who still has this existential wisdom? It looks as if one is not even allowed to speak about it. Is this still a taboo?

The purpose of this book is twofold: first, to put the mystical essence of life into words as clearly as possible; and second, to guide you on several paths to enlightenment. The source for this is the mystical knowledge of ancient India, as revealed by their 'Rishis', sages.

Should you have any doubts about whether you will be able to fathom the mystical secret to be revealed, please understand this: the fact that you have this book in your hands shows that you have an interest in spirituality. As the so-called secret is hidden in your own soul, all you need to do is to listen quietly to my words, and the recognition of their meaning will arise from within by itself. When you try to put the spiritual concepts you are about to discover into practice, although it won't always be easy, please keep in mind that every effort has its value.

In Part I of this book, the foundation necessary for understanding mysticism is provided. Because the Eastern way of thinking seems totally different from our Western way of thinking, we will make a bridge between East and West. The limits of reasoning are also explained. Next, the meaning of the term 'enlightenment' is explained, as well as the enormous importance of insight into Reality. Then insight into Reality is built up in four steps. In the process, the concept of 'time' is also investigated. From an enlightened point of view, time does not exist. Reality is not bound by time or place. It is the eternal 'now'.

The use of the word 'Reality' is essential. Mystics use this to emphasize that the realization of the Absolute (or whatever synonym is used), is not a fiction or a hallucination. No, the 'experience of oneness with the Absolute' means an intense, existential 'now' experience. Any description of this is inadequate. To those who have had an experience like this, perhaps the following description will be meaningful. It is the experience of 'the fullness of the void!'

In Part II of this book, the most essential philosophy of the ancient Rishis of India, called Advaita Vedanta, is studied. Learning to distinguish between that which is absolute and that which is relative is the basis for understanding mysticism and enlightenment. In order to grow in the understanding of this, meditation is necessary. Although there are many different meditation techniques, I limited myself to the method belonging to Advaita Vedanta. This is meditation directly on the own Self, because that is where the distinction between the Absolute and the relative has to unfold.

Part III looks at two other very old Hindu philosophies: Samkhya and Tantra. In the section on Tantra, an attempt is made to explain the mystery of sexuality in relation to enlightenment. When sexuality is understood and experienced as the life energy with which the Absolute manifests itself in our being, the vision of the Absolute (Reality) may arise.

In Part IV, I use a totally different approach. Here, I explain the way to enlightenment through our daily life. It is essential in all our spiritual practice to see through the nature of the ego. This is so important because it is our ego, as the scriptures (and Gurus) teach us that prevents us from seeing Reality as it is.

Even if we are able to live in the world with a 'thin' ego, we still have to cope with the daily struggle for life, where we are constantly confronted with other egos. Understanding how to deal with the ego is good, but putting the knowledge in actual practice is often very difficult.

I would still like to invite you to give this a serious try. The stressful ego, which we are afraid of losing, should not be what really matters to us. Some courage is required to give up the false image that we want to keep up for others. If we manage to achieve this, however, the basic cause of stress and other mental suffering falls away. That which was so hard to give up is of little value compared to what you will find within yourself.

To protect you on this spiritual path through daily life, I will show you the way to maintain the necessary balance between living in the world with a thin ego and preserving and developing your spirituality.

Part V gives an explanation of the mystery of enlightenment through devotion to the Divine, which is pure love. In this, too, the Absolute is realized as the highest Reality. In the end, knowledge (Jnana) and devotion (Bhakti) lead to the same initiation into Reality. The Absolute is God. The impersonal and the personal aspect of transcendental Reality turn out to be one and the same Self. We see a testimony of this in the description of the life and vision of the Hindu Saint Sri Ramakrishna.

Finally, I would like to suggest that you do not read these texts as you would read a book. Consider the words to be spoken slowly and to you in person.

I sincerely hope that with this book I give you something that brings you much wisdom and happiness.

Part I

Basics of the
Ancient Universal Hindu Wisdom

1.01 Introduction

Thousands of years before the beginning of our era, long before writing was invented, the Hindu wisdom was passed on orally from generation to generation. Just imagine: many old cultures, such as those of the Egyptians, Mayans, Incas, Aztecs, Greeks, and Romans no longer exist, nor have they for a very long time.

But the ancient Hindu wisdom, where the inner secret is hidden in its profound philosophy called 'Yoga' (to 'yoke' together) has its roots in even earlier times, and it still exists. This alone should make it worth trying to deepen our knowledge of this ancient wisdom.

Coming to know the Yoga philosophy may seem to be simple. You can read a few books, take a course in Yoga, or even go to India. In this way, you will discover easily why Yoga has survived all this time, and still has such an appeal for so many people.

But, no—it is not as simple as that. The Yoga we would learn about that way is only the outside shell, the surface of a secret mystic path that belongs to a culture which is not ours. If we want to avoid losing interest because of such a superficial introduction, we must first try to bridge the differences in spiritual thinking between the East and the West.

When we realize that our Western way of thinking is less different from the Oriental way than we thought, it will be easier for us to go deeper into the mystical Oriental secret.

1.02 East and West Can Meet

One of the most significant differences between the East and the West, centers on religion. Just compare Hinduism with our Christian tradition. In Hinduism, there are many gods and goddesses. In Christianity, we have one God. In Hinduism, one believes in reincarnation and rebirth. In Christianity, one believes in resurrection from death. Hinduism has the caste system, while Christianity celebrates the idea of love for our neighbor.

These characteristics may seem contradictory, but we can bridge these differences by understanding that Hinduism considers its gods and goddesses simply as a number of aspects of one spiritual principle, which are pictured as (super) human entities to make these aspects clear to the believer.

Both the concepts of reincarnation and resurrection from death refer to the immortality of the soul.

As far as the caste system is concerned, this originally just distinguished the different social levels in society, just as we still distinguish them in our Western society, to a certain extent. However, in actual practice, this system has evolved throughout the centuries into a social straitjacket unacceptable to us in the West. The Christian concept of love for our neighbor seems much more 'human' to us— but, with us too, practice does not always match up to theory.

Another difference between the religions of the Hindus and the West is the relationship between man and the Supreme Being. The worship in the East of gods and goddesses, saints and gurus (teachers), seems odd to us, but makes sense. Through the object of devotion, one can make contact with that aspect of the divine, from which that deity or saint is an expression. In other words, it is possible to make contact with or achieve a relationship with the divine, with God, through the object of worship or veneration.

In Hinduism, it has always been assumed that a connection between the human being and the Supreme Being is possible. Here in the West, this seems quite different. The traditional point of view in general is: man is a sinful being here below, and God is unknowable—far away, somewhere high above. But someone who understands what Jesus has said very well knows that 'The kingdom of heaven is within you'.

Turn within and you will discover the truth about God and what this means for you, inside yourself. So here too, just as I mentioned earlier, differences at first sight turn out to be, on closer inspection, basically no differences at all.

1.03 Sacred Knowledge Needs to be Protected
Although we can bridge these apparent differences in this way,

and already begin to grasp more of the significance of Yoga, there is another point that will make it difficult to get to the very heart of the Yoga philosophy. Even in Hinduism, this mystical essence often stays hidden.

From way back, as in other mystical traditions, one has always handled the essence of mysticism very cautiously. The Guru, or teacher, hands over his knowledge preferably only to those who are worthy to possess that knowledge. The circle of insiders will not easily accept outsiders. The reason for this is that this mystic knowledge is regarded as so precious that it has to be prevented from being used badly or possibly abused as an 'interesting philosophy' by less serious people.

We Westerners can fill books full of philosophies and invent beautiful theoretical solutions and explanations, without living in accordance with our theories. For the Yoga mystic, the yogi, this is different. The secret wisdom is only to be given to those who are able to live by it.

This is why many Western seekers, who have tried in the past to fathom the secrets of India, ended at a closed door. For the Indian, theory and practice must be the same. We in the West seem to be a bit more casual about this.

1.04 Man's Most Important Relationship

Trusting that we have sufficiently bridged the differences between the East and the West, and that the reader can accept the knowledge that will be revealed with respect, we will now talk about the essence of the mystical Yoga doctrine.

I have indicated that the possibility of a relationship between man and the Supreme Being is to be found in both Eastern and Western cultures. In the East, all aspects of religion are an expression of the assumed relationship between man and God. In our culture, however, man seems separated from a presumed God somewhere high above. But anyone who looks more deeply into our Christian religion will also find references to divinity in man.

This relationship between man and God must now be the subject of discussion, for this is what it's all about.

First of all, when we use that little word 'God', who knows what we mean? Some people say that God did not create man, but that man created God. By this, they mean that man creates his own version of what the Supreme Being might be, and then calls himself religious when he believes in his own projections and ideas about God. In this way, all kinds of qualities—goodness, fairness and forgiveness—are attributed to God, but God is also seen as strict and at times angry. There are also people who say: 'Although we don't know God, we do know His word, through the Bible and through His Son, Jesus Christ. Who or what God is, we may never know, but God's word is enough'. So, in both situations, whether you make your own impression about God or not, he remains unknown.

The criteria for believing or not believing has then simply become: you want to believe in God, therefore you believe (as mentioned above); or, you can't believe in God, therefore you don't believe (the atheistic view). Would it not be wiser then, because we have no knowledge of what we are talking about, not to use this little word 'God' for the time being?

There are also many people who say: 'I do believe there is something, but what exactly, I really don't know'. In this case, Yoga teaches us that indeed there is 'something', but this 'something' cannot be grasped by our power of reasoning.

'Yes, but that's not going to get me anywhere,' you might say. 'That I already knew. When something cannot be grasped by our power of reasoning, what's the use of philosophizing about it any further?' In answer to this, the Yoga doctrine tells us that although that unknown 'something' is hidden from us now, it is possible to discover it. What is now covered can be uncovered.

And when this uncovering—this revelation, as you might call it—occurs, it turns out to be of such significance that it surpasses in importance anything you have experienced before.

'Look,' says the Hindu sage, the spiritual teacher, 'if you will now just think along with me, then you will see that in the end it is absolutely logical that there is 'something', and that the realization of this something is of tremendous importance for you as a human being.'

1.05 By the Perceptible Reality to the Ultimate Reality
Listen carefully—we are going to take four steps, and if you pay attention as we walk then I expect that after the fourth step you will say, 'Yes—that's it!'

The first step
Observe the world around you and you will find that everything that exists is subject to change at all times. Nothing at this moment is exactly the same as it was the moment before, or will be in the next moment. Everything in nature is constantly changing. In man, in yourself, you may see this change less clearly than in a flower, but it is not difficult to see that everything that exists is subject to change, and always goes through a stage of appearing and disappearing. Don't think that this applies only for living things. A building which is not maintained, for instance, will collapse one day. And even a mountain (we cannot imagine anything more solid), will weather and erode. That's why in geology one can speak of old and young mountains. Change is always underway, no matter how slowly or imperceptibly. This change is something man wants to measure—and his tool of measurement is called… time.

Time applies to everything that is temporary. Beyond this, time does not exist. Just as there are no miles and pounds, there are no hours or minutes. These concepts are just tools to measure distance, weight, and change, respectively.

So, there is no such thing as time. We just experience it because we ourselves are temporary. We are subject to change, which we can measure, thanks to the concept of time.

Perhaps one day people will realize that time does not exist at all, just as long ago people accepted that the earth was round and revolved around the sun, after having believed it was flat and the center of the universe. There is only 'change in the unchangeable', the eternal Now, Reality.

This insight into the illusion of time is essential, and further on the reader will learn the importance of the distinction between the timeless and the temporary.

Meanwhile, back to the first step!

Everything that exists is subject to change. This change does not happen chaotically. Everything happens according to fixed laws of nature—for example, the inherent order in the total process of life and the multiplication of life. What physical and spiritual growth is not repeated again and again, in fixed patterns, in each human being? There are many areas in which we can see the relationship between cause and effect. Think of all the decisions you have made in your life; for example, your choice of life partner, career, or religion. Consider all the effects of these choices (causes), many of them lasting for many years!

Cause and effect create a chain of effects that are related to one another. Considering this chain of cause and effect, it is not difficult to see that we and the world as it appears today are a result, an outcome of everything that has happened in the past. For the philosopher, this raises the question: what is the primal cause—what is the origin of all this? Where did this all start? Logically, there should be something, but what?

It is more logical to suppose that there is a primal cause than to say that there is no cause. When we deny that there is a primal cause, we are only saying that we cannot find a primal cause, and that everything came into being by coincidence. But even then the question arises: 'Coincidence caused by what?'

On the other hand, every primal cause that we might invent intellectually cannot by definition be the primal cause because, for any cause that we might find, we can ask: 'And where does that come from?'

This is a complex problem, which we can only solve by

considering the following: according to the law of cause and effect there must be a primal cause. But, this cause cannot be a material one and is therefore not perceptible. If it were, it could never be the primal cause because, by its very existence, it would by necessity have its own preceding cause.

So, as the primal cause is not material, it will not be subject to change (time). This means that it has been in the past, is in the present and shall be in the future.

To summarize the first step: the continuous process of change (as seen in life and matter) is necessarily founded on a primal (timeless) cause—which is, by definition, non-material.

The second step
In everything that changes, energy is active. Look at man, animals, and plants. Food is converted into life's energy, which enables us to grow and function. Energy drives everything. Some scientists say that 'everything is energy'. To the philosopher, of course, the question will arise: where does this energy come from? It cannot be the primal cause, because energy too must have an origin.

If we forget about the origin of energy for a moment and examine energy, as such, then we can conclude that energy is a blind force. By this I mean that energy is a non-conscious force. Take fire, for example; you can warm your home with it or burn your home down with it. Then there's nuclear energy; this can provide the whole world with electric energy, or destroy the whole world. Or, you can use your own energy to save someone from drowning in the sea, or you can throw him into it. In other words, it is our conscious mind that decides how to use energy. Energy itself does not think. It is not conscious—it is simply a blind force.

From this too, one can conclude that energy cannot be the primal cause. One would be more inclined to think that energy is the means, the instrument, by which the unknown primal cause can manifest itself. This brings us to the third insight.

The third step

Simply put, something that appears from somewhere must have been there before. Or, everything that came into being from the timeless primal cause, logically and in principle, must have been potentially present before. This means that the unknown, creative principle has in itself the possibility of manifesting everything that exists, has existed, and will exist. This creative principle: could it be possible that it is blind, non-consciousness, just as energy is?

This seems impossible—and illogical, too—in the context of the whole creation. It is easy to see how miraculously and how ingeniously everything is 'constructed', and the extent of its complexity. Consider the human body, with all its organs and nerves. Look at the whole of nature. If the primal cause were to be blind, not conscious, no form of life whatsoever could have developed. There must be 'something' that develops, mustn't there? The whole problem with getting a hold on this line of reasoning is that our reasoning is also 'secondary' to that unknown primal cause.

When we try to explain ourselves and the whole creation, and we want to look for that non-material primal cause, we can reason 'backwards' as far as the 'not something', the non-material, the space in which everything came into being. This is because everything has been manifested in that void, and is therefore secondary to it. Our intellect—our brains—also came into being in that space, and therefore we will never be able to fathom intellectually the essence of space.

If you still want to try it, let us think about that concept of space. If we should leave earth and find ourselves in space, we would not fall or rise, because there are no 'below and above' (there is no gravity, as we say). If there were no space—universe, that is—with all the stars and planets, what would there be then? Theoretically, space must also have an end, but what lies beyond? As you see, our thinking comes to an end at the void—space—in which the whole universe appeared. Still, nothing is more real than that space in which the universe appears.

I emphasize this to show that in our search for the truth (primal cause) of life, reasoning brings us to 'nothingness'—the void. We cannot go any further.

If, however, we want to continue our line of reasoning, we have to accept this limitation in our ability to understand the 'non material, timeless, eternal primal cause'. At this point, we can do no more than say that the unknowable primal cause cannot be non-conscious, but has to be conscious.

You may wonder whether this conclusion is really so important. Well, we are not there yet. This run-up was necessary to be able to understand the final conclusion—which we are about to examine.

The fourth step

Of all the millions of living species, there is one that distinguishes itself fundamentally from the others—the human being. What makes man so special compared to all other species of life? It is the fact that man is conscious, i.e. conscious of him/herself!

At the third step, we concluded that the primal cause has to be conscious. Now we are saying that man is conscious. So we have found a resemblance between the primal cause and man. That from which everything originates and man, are both conscious. Do you know how this reality, this truth, is worded in the Bible?

'God created Man in His own image.'

What a discovery! Now we can understand this statement. The resemblance between God and man is: just as God as primal cause is conscious, so man is conscious. God gave man His own image (essence).

In this resemblance, the secret of life, the mystery of mysticism is hidden. We heard the statement, 'God created man in His own image' long ago. But until now we probably did not know how to interpret it. Through reasoning based on the visible reality, we came to the conclusion that there is a similarity, a resemblance, between man and his origin—Reality.

16

1.06 Enlightenment Means Experiencing Reality

The conclusion that there is a similarity between man and his origin is a very important one. This immediately raises the question of the meaning of this similarity. Is this just a theoretical observation, or does it also have spiritual or practical consequences?

The Yoga philosophy—and, in fact, any true religion—claims that it is possible to discover this similarity within yourself. This similarity is always there. It just needs to be discovered. And this discovering does not mean just giving an explanation, as I am doing here. There is much more to it. This similarity can really be experienced, lived. And this is what it is all about.

When we experience our oneness with that which precedes everything, with the primal cause—or whatever name we use for the 'great unknown'—then we become seers and we know that what always is: Reality. This insight makes it very clear that this infinite primal cause, this omnipresent Reality, is the source of all that is. Someone who has this insight is called 'enlightened'. Being enlightened can now be defined as having insight into Reality.

1.07 Reality Became You and Me

Someone who has this insight knows that the worldly, common reality is temporary and relative compared with 'That' (Reality), from which everything came into existence. This 'knowing' of the origin of life is therefore not based on a religious dogma like 'God created everything'. No, this knowing means that 'That' is seen and experienced.

In the experience of enlightenment, one sees that the real Self (behind ego), is the same as (one with) the omnipresent, primal cause, the Absolute. It means fully understanding that 'I am That'— or the other way round: 'That has become the human being that I am.'

Man has come into life by and in that which is eternal. He can be called a cosmic design, a cosmic creation. He has a body and within the body feelings, emotions and consciousness. And the clearer this consciousness, the more of the essence, the Absolute, radiates from him. Man is the Absolute. The Absolute has become man. It is this achievement of insight into Reality, which is the final goal of Yoga.

1.08 Yoga: To Unite with Reality

The word 'Yoga' derives from the Sanskrit (the ancient Hindu language) word *Yug*, which means yoke, to unify, to bring together. This means that the ancient Hindus give us instructions, through their Yoga 'method', on how to attain a conscious experience of the oneness of man and the Absolute. I use the word 'Absolute' on purpose. It is neutral, not colored, because we have to avoid putting our human projections on what, for the time being, is the unknown primal cause.

Self-realization, as we call this insight into Reality, is of immeasurable value. Before I elaborate on this, let me say something about the principles of Yoga in general, followed by a brief explanation of the main Yoga systems. To put it simply, the purpose of all the different Yoga systems is to gain control over one's thoughts (mind). In the end, that's what this is all about. It is one's thoughts (in total called the ego), which block the awareness of the Absolute.

1.09 We Are More Than Our Thoughts

I think this simple information about our thoughts in the preceding paragraph requires clarification. In general, people believe that we are like we think. We all have our own thoughts, and these thoughts shape our unique personality. To a certain extent, this is correct, but if we look carefully, we realize that we *are* not our thoughts, but we *have* our thoughts. We can be *aware* of our thoughts. These thoughts 'appear' in us. The fact that our thoughts appear in us must lead to the understanding that 'if my thoughts appear in me, then I cannot be my thoughts, but must be the 'THAT' in which my thoughts do appear. And what is the 'THAT' in which my thoughts appear?' The answer is: awareness—self-awareness.

This awareness is something we all know. We are that awareness, but we do not always realize this, because this clarity is constantly clouded by our thoughts, just as clouds cover the sun's brightness.

The reason for this 'eclipse of the sun' in us is that we unconsciously identify ourselves with our thoughts. This means that our attention is not conscious enough, and because of a lack of spiritual information and training, it stays attached to our thoughts. We are hypnotized—spellbound—by our personal interpretation of the outside world.

The problem with this 'thinking' of ours is that it is very much overestimated. We do not realize that our thinking and reasoning are simply tools. We can use these tools for everything that can be solved intellectually—for example, to design houses or computer programs, to do research as a scientist, or just to earn our daily bread. For these kinds of things we are equipped with our 'thinking tool'. However, just as a carpenter does not identify with his hammer and a driver knows he is not his car, so we must realize who we are. We are not our changeable 'thinking equipment'.

This is what I mean when I say that our reasoning is overestimated. However practical and necessary it is, our reasoning—our intellect—is limited. The insight into our true identity arises in a territory outside the sphere of our thinking.

If you are not used to bothering yourself with this kind of thing, you may think it a strange idea that you can be aware of yourself without thinking something. Still, when you turn your attention inward, you will see that this is possible.

Obviously, this won't mean that we are instantly enlightened and able to fathom the reality of our existence. To stop the endless inner stream of thoughts and to discover the Absolute in your own consciousness requires more. In fact, a slow but complete change must take place in you. For this reason, India's ancient seers developed different ways to help people in their struggle for insight into Reality—because obtaining this insight was considered to be nothing less than the reason for living. These different ways all have the same goal—insight into/realization of Reality. This means understanding: you are That (the timeless Reality), and That has become you.

The condition for attaining this insight is always 'thought' (the mind), has to calm down, brought under control. In this way, self-awareness becomes clearer and clearer, and space is created where the understanding of the unity behind all that exists can grow.

1.10 Outlines of the Four Traditional Yoga Ways to Enlightenment

Best known to us in the West is the Hatha Yoga. In this system, physical posture, a better way of breathing, and a way to experience a conscious complete relaxation, are taught. The combination of these three aspects aims to achieve an optimal condition of body and mind. If taught properly (there is no pressure to become an acrobat, a pair of bellows, or a clairvoyant), then peace will arise in the mind of the student. This peace can be the foundation on which everything that is good in man—and even Self-realization—can grow. Hatha Yoga is in fact a part of Raja Yoga (Royal Yoga).

Raja Yoga

This system consists of eight parts, together aiming at the complete transformation of man:

1. Yama: five guidelines for what not to do (use violence, lie, steal, be indecent, be desirous)
2. Niyama: five guidelines for what to do (be pure, be contented, be independent of pain and pleasure, study the scriptures, surrender to God)
3. Asana: physical exercises (postures, Hatha Yoga)
4. Pranayama: breathing exercises (Hatha Yoga)
5. Pratyahara: withdrawing the senses from outward objects (for relaxation, Hatha Yoga)
6. Dharana: training to concentrate the mind

7. Dhyana: meditation, being effortlessly one with the subject of meditation
8. Samadhi: experiencing oneness with the Absolute, Reality, God, one's true Self.

As these concepts of Raja Yoga were formulated 'only' some hundreds of years B.C. (by Patanjali) and we engage ourselves exclusively in the ancient Hindu wisdom, I will not explain this Raja Yoga any further in this book.

Jnana Yoga

Jnana means knowledge. This path aims to guide us to Reality by means of right knowledge. This does not mean that we can realize Reality by reasoning only. I explained the limitations of reasoning earlier. Knowledge in this context means that by reflecting seriously on some specific spiritual aspects of life, the knowledge obtained in this way should become the inspiration for practicing a natural meditation, which precedes Self-realization.

These specific spiritual aspects of life could be the four steps, as explained in section 1.05, followed by the exercise of distinguishing the relative from the Absolute. Another way to obtain knowledge in order to prepare for meditation is to study religious scriptures— such as the Bhagavad Gita, Upanishads, Ramayana, or others.

In addition to these 'exercises', some further basic philosophical concepts have to be understood, and with these concepts one can study the most important philosophy of Jnana Yoga—the Advaita Vedanta, or the philosophy of non-duality.

Through Advaita Vedanta, one comes to know what is really essential for understanding life, and this makes one look inside instead of only outside. By doing so, the ego—thought—is overcome, and this makes it possible for the true 'human being' to come forth. Then we can speak of 'natural meditation', because it is our true nature to be bright and conscious of our self. The way back home, to our 'primal state' still exists. However, we need to be guided by a philosophy like Advaita Vedanta to find our way. Jnana Yoga will be treated in greater detail in part two of this book.

Karma Yoga

This is the path of growing toward insight into Reality through right action. The essence is that acting in ways that are good prevails over our selfish wants. And good is that which is in harmony with 'Dharma', the natural spiritual laws of life. Dharma is a very profound concept, which we shall discuss in more detail in Part IV. The main thought is that man should grow up in love, live life in accordance with his/her nature and talents, and be inspired by spiritual knowledge. In this way, one should be able to merge into the Absolute, which is pure love, when life comes to an end.

If we follow the path of Karma Yoga, we try for ourselves and those for whom we are responsible—children, parents, partner, fellow citizens, etc.—to live a life in harmony with Dharma. If we do this seriously, we will overcome our ego(ism), because we live a disciplined life, in tune with the spiritual laws of life. In this way, inner peace grows, which is the basis for Self-realization.

As an example of such a way of life, we can mention Mother Teresa, who lived in India for many years. This Catholic nun took in dying people from the street and tried to open them to the love of the Absolute to which they were to return, by making them feel loved in their final hours. She said that she saw Jesus Christ, the Absolute, in those dying people. This example may seem somewhat extreme and in her spiritual life there must have been more than just the 'conquest of egoism'. And what this 'more' was brings us to the fourth main path of Yoga.

Bhakti Yoga

It is very natural that the path of Karma Yoga changes gradually into that of Bhakti Yoga. This path too requires an offering up of the worldly ego to that which surpasses the limitations of time and place. The way of Bhakti means the way of devotion to the Absolute, the Reality, which is to be realized. Because devotion directly to the Absolute is usually not possible, one must first search for a Guru, or for an image or something else that evokes associations of the Divine for the devotee, to direct ones devotion to.

When thinking about the example of Mother Teresa, one can understand how she, through her devotion to Jesus as an intermediary between man and Reality, attained Self-realization and reached God. Her seeing Jesus—Reality—in suffering human beings, can be seen as proof of her knowing of God (nevertheless, she herself said that she did not experience God all the time in her life).

The essence of to what or whom the Bhakti yogi gives devotion is to be discovered in his/her own Self. By conquering the ego, the uncontrolled mind, this true Self can be realized.

Bhakti Yoga and Karma Yoga will also be covered in more detail further on in this book.

1.11 The Importance of the Realization of Reality
After this brief explanation of the main paths to insight into Reality, as taught by the ancient Hindu sages, I will explain the significance and the consequences of the realization of Reality.

First of all, it will be clear that for all people who are looking for a deeper meaning of life, this wisdom gives a route description toward the ultimate goal. In the preface of this book I stated that everybody has the longing to rediscover his or her 'source' deep inside, although one isn't necessarily aware of this. It will be clear that simply 'being along the way' already gives a sense of satisfaction. Take Hatha Yoga, for example. Following this method, one experiences strength, calmness, and ultimately the disappearance of stress. This is even more strongly felt when one treads the other paths. But, just to start, to find the 'entrance,' is not all that easy, because we are blocked by our ego.

If you do manage to get started on the way, you will notice that changes are taking place. These can be many, and different in nature.

In the next parts, you will come across some of these changes.

So, what is the significance of living from Reality? Living from Reality means living in 'the timeless'. Enlightened people have described this as 'achieving immortality'. This way of putting it is quite correct, because that which one has realized oneself to be is not subject to birth or death (as the body is). 'That' always is, cannot not be.

Achieving immortality, therefore, does not mean that one thinks to exist physically or as a person forever. In this context, insight into Reality means that one has realized that one is in essence not the body nor the personality, but 'That' which always is. The enlightened one sees this essence as his inner Self (beyond the ego), and he also sees that all that lives has the same essence (Reality) as its source.

A consequence of this insight is a very special attitude toward the surrounding world. Since the Absolute, that which can be indicated as all that is good, peace, fullness, and one without a second, is seen as ever-manifesting, the enlightened one can only adapt himself spontaneously to Dharma, the way of living in accordance with the natural spiritual laws of life. Everything that contradicts Dharma is seen as deviating from Reality—as negative. The enlightened one sees clearly that to live toward Reality makes us happy, because such a life corresponds with our true nature.

Haven't we all had the experience that, even if we don't know much about philosophy or religion, we feel much happier if we have a positive attitude toward life instead of a negative one? This is already an indication. Your original state is positive, and this belongs to you.

To live from the timeless, from eternity, also means that the search for the meaning of life has come to an end. The enlightened one has come to a standstill in the unchangeable.

External life, however, possibly apparently unchanged, continues. But the problems the average man or woman has to face, like loneliness, the urge to achieve, fear, and many other negative things, have no further meaning for the enlightened one. One can say that the sage has passed beyond the world of duality and contradiction. All relative things are seen against the background of that which always, eternally is, in which the sage has his/her roots and experiences Reality, unity, and happiness.

1.12 Why Is There So Much Misery?

A very important question now has to be asked and answered. How do all these beautiful concepts we are talking about relate to all the misery that is found in the world? The answer is that all disasters other than natural ones—that is wars, environmental destruction, economic exploitation, etc.—are all 'man's work'. Humanity in general is apparently not aware of Reality as I explain it. If it were, humanity would, as I said earlier, naturally adapt to Dharma, and we would have a totally different past and present.

The sages say about this that man is ignorant. It is this all penetrating ignorance that is the primal cause of the suffering of mankind. All the (many) good things that happen in the lives of people who do not necessarily know Reality, happen when they are just able to be themselves. This self, you see, is good and the less we stray from our true nature, the more we will spontaneously behave positively.

1.13 What Is the Main Cause of Human Ignorance About Reality?

Just what is the cause of this so-called ignorance? In Christianity, one says that it is man's original sin (Fall) that made him forget God. With this, we usually think of our falling for our sexual desires (the story of Adam and Eve). That's a pity, because however much misery is caused by our misinterpretation of sexuality, the main cause of our ignorance is another inborn inclination—egoism. In the end, everything that's bad, all the harm we cause each other and our environment, results from egoism.

This egoism, which after all is our survival instinct, is rooted deeply in everyone, so we might actually say that it cannot be bad. And indeed, in essence, egoism is not bad. It is the 'I-sense' that makes us human. But, with the 'I'—the ego—we can look at two directions. We can look inside and outside. If we only look outside, we become obsessed by the world around us and, lacking information regarding our true nature, we get entangled in it. The more we lose our awareness of what we really are, the more we become a caricature of the qualities which accidentally prevail. This will irrevocably create an egoistic attitude in the negative sense.

When we look inside, meditate regularly (and who will do that when not trained to), our ego will be transformed gradually into purer and purer self-awareness, ending with the realization of our oneness with the Absolute, as a mark that we have become truly human. So the main cause of human ignorance about Reality is that man does not rise above the level of egoism and therefore remains blinded by the material world.

1.14 Any Effort Will Have its Value

Throughout the centuries, there have always been people, in all great cultures, who have fathomed the mystery of existence in themselves. It is my deepest conviction that if there is anything the world needs in this age, it is that humanity changes its materialistic way of life into a spiritual one. Only from inside, from the heart, can an essential positive change arise—and not from our reasoning, however intellectual this may seem.

Should you think that this would be too difficult, consider the following: we can each choose to do something about it—or not. If we don't, the outcome is certain. If we do, anything is possible. Just remember—if we become wiser, humanity has become wiser, because *we are humanity!*

Part II

Everything That Exists Originates from ONE

2.01 Introduction

Long ago, before the invention of writing, sacred knowledge was passed on orally. If you have ever relayed a message by whispering it in the ear of your neighbor, you will know how little of the original message remains intact after only a few whisperers.

Imagine then, orally passing on a complete mystical tradition for thousands of years! This required some very special 'skills'—such as very pithy phrasing and repeating over and over again, to make the necessary 'soul to soul' communication possible. In this spirit of repetition, please allow me to briefly summarize what we have covered thus far.

There is no human being in the world, no animal, no plant— literally nothing in the world—that came into being by itself. Man is ignorant of the fact that he is an expression of a 'cosmic, conscious, creative principle'. This unknown primal cause has become all that lives—including us, as human beings. The Absolute became man, and man is (from) the Absolute. The achievement of insight into this primal cause (Reality) is called 'enlightenment'. To live from the timeless eternity, which is being enlightened, means to live above all duality, above all opposites. Searching has come to an end, and 'spirit' has become manifest in the material. The human being has reached its destiny.

The cause of all negative 'man's work' in the world is the general ignorance about Reality (the Absolute). This ignorance is a result of a lack of knowledge about the ego, the 'I' of man. Because of the absence of correct spiritual education, man's attention is fragmentized. This happens because of the continuous identification with the inexhaustible stream of thoughts. The mind is turned outward, and because of this, the true human is not manifested as he could be.

In ancient times, people in India knew how to live in order to manifest the original, true spiritual nature of man. Their mystical knowledge resided in their Yoga philosophy. In this treasury, different spiritual ways are 'stored', all leading to the same goal: to become one, to unify (yoke) the individual consciousness with the cosmic consciousness—that is to say, to realize Reality.

The four best-known Yoga Ways were introduced very briefly in Part I. They are Jnana Yoga, Raja Yoga (of which Hatha Yoga is a part), Karma Yoga, and Bhakti Yoga. It is not a question of choosing one of these ways and having enlightenment follows automatically. On the contrary, the seeker investigates the different possible ways. What does not appeal is left aside, while what remains is investigated more deeply and absorbed. Perhaps then the search can be continued. In the course of the process, we could conclude that we have chosen the way of devotion. The yogi calls this 'Bhakti'. Or we can work on ourselves by serving other people, in which case we are talking about Karma Yoga. Or, beginning with Hatha Yoga, we try to live according to the principle of a healthy mind in a healthy body. Gradually, we train ourselves in concentration and meditation, along the path of Raja Yoga.

If we have a philosophical turn of mind, we try to proceed rationally as far as possible. If this happens in the right way, and in combination with meditation on the self—introspection—then we speak of Jnana Yoga.

Usually, when people want more depth in their lives and they start to investigate the Indian wisdom, they each follow their own combination of these four main paths. As I see it, Yoga is not a typical Eastern affair. We can adapt the concepts to our own way of thinking very easily. In fact, every human being follows his own path of spiritual growth in his life—even if one is not conscious of this. Only a few are aware of the fact that there is a destination to reach, and that working toward the realization of that destination in one's daily life is the most meaningful thing one can do.

2.02 'God Created Man in His Own Image'
Now we will look specifically at Jnana Yoga. First, the Jnani (a rationalist) has become convinced that there is 'something' that must be discovered, or realized. This conviction that there must

be that something is essential to all Yoga—in fact, to all religion, to all mysticism. In the first part, we set up a reasoning that revealed a necessary present conscious primal cause, which always is and cannot *not* be. The four steps were, in brief:

1. Everything that exists is always subject to change.
2. In all that changes, energy is active. This energy is a non-conscious force, which has to be preceded by an invisible primal cause.
3. Anything that appears out of something (the primal cause) must have been in that something before; in other words, the primal, timeless, permanent cause is a source of endless creativity. This source cannot be non-conscious, blind.
4. Man is also not non-conscious, and in this resembles the timeless primal cause.

So there is a similarity, an equality between man and his origin. Long ago (in the Bible) this was expressed as: 'God created man in His Own image'. This image is consciousness.

So by following this or a similar line of reasoning, the Jnani is confident, that he, as a human being, is a manifestation, an expression, of a conscious cosmic creative principle. And he knows that he can realize (come to know) this cosmic absolute principle through inner (spiritual) development.

Seekers who think that they can become enlightened through the intellect alone must understand that knowledge alone is not enough. The next step for someone who wants to follow the path of the Jnani is to investigate and try to realize (understand) the distinction between the Absolute and the relative.

2.03 Seeing Through Relativity is Necessary

We usually live completely in the sphere of the relative—that is, the transitory, temporal—world. This is the level of differences, the world of duality. We have to see through the relativity of this way of being. All the things we normally worry about are, strictly speaking, relative, which means temporary. By this I mean things that exist, but could also not exist. I am referring to things such as human relationships, earning our daily bread, our leisure activities, diseases, and all the other things that attract or require our attention: in short, our daily reality. If we are unable to see through the relativity (transitoriness) of this daily reality, we will become absorbed in it and, in the end, drown in it. By this I mean that if we have always nourished our minds with passing 'important things', the meaning of our lives will not become clear to us, and at the end our conscious will fade away unsatisfied and restless.

2.04 The Absolute

a) The Eternal NOW

Well then, what is the Absolute that has to be distinguished from the relative? As I have said before, it is not possible to understand Reality, the Absolute, with the mind. What I can do is point to it, in the hope that you will see it yourself.

First of all, one has to understand that the awareness of the Absolute has two aspects: 'It' (the Absolute) is to be 'seen' at the same time outside (transcendent) as well as inside yourself (immanent).

With regard to the transcendent aspect, contemplate your own appearing and disappearing against the background of that which does not come and go, but always is, that in which you appear and disappear. That background—that Reality—is that which always is and cannot not be. It is the 'Omnipresent Being'—the Absolute. An enlightened person might call it 'awareness, clearness, or presence'.

With regard to the immanent aspect of the Absolute, the 'seer' of the Absolute experiences that his (inner) Self *is* that transcendent Reality, *is* happiness or absolute quietness, peace and love. Very close too comes the expression, 'the Self is silence'. The Self is a conscious, perfect rest emanating... Silence. This silence is not disturbed by restless thoughts. Of this conscious, quiet inner experience, one can say, 'It is... now.'—it is the 'perfect moment'. As this Absolute is timeless, we can say, when we recognize this perfect moment, 'It is the eternal... NOW!' The 'eternal now' seems like a contradiction, but it is not. That perfect moment always *IS* but we, because of our thoughts, are not always there. Sadly, we are perhaps almost never there.

b) To Fathom the 'Great Void' Is Not Possible

Well, what more can we say about that Absolute, that eternal NOW? What can we say about the 'great void'—which, according to mystics, is the 'ultimate fullness?'

- It IS and cannot *not* be (is Absolute)
- All life originates from it, is sustained by it, and will return to it (in Hindu terminology it is Brahma, Vishnu and Shiva)
- It is unchanging and therefore timeless (not born and immortal)
- It is everywhere and not somewhere (everywhere and nowhere)
- If it were not, nothing could be there (first that and then all the rest)
- That is Reality (the Hindu mantra Om Tat Sat)
- That has become you (the mantra Tat Tvam Asi)
- I am *that* in my deepest being (the mantra Aham Brahmasmi)

We could carry on like this for a while, but this should be enough. Here, we directly touch the mystery of mysticism. What is said is true, but if you have no insight into it yet, it will be difficult to grasp. Therefore, let us try now to say something about the nature of the Absolute.

c) The Relationship Between the Absolute and the Human Soul

To start with, what is the relationship between the Absolute and the human soul? This relationship is investigated in the Vedanta philosophy. In Vedanta there are three points of view concerning this relationship:

1 Total identity of the human soul and the Absolute (non-duality, Advaita Vedanta)
2 Unity, but no identity of the human soul and the Absolute (Visisht Advaita)
3 The Absolute as God, separated from man (Dvaita Vedanta).

It is not my intention to discuss these points of view in detail in this book. But I do want to guide you through these 'complementary' points of view, in order to make you understand how the reasoning of the ancient Hindu sages can lead to the insight into ultimate Reality.

If someone has not yet found God, he/she will—if religious—believe that God is 'somewhere' outside of him/her (the third point of view). As God is not known, the two other points of view mentioned above will have no meaning for him/her.

Amazing, isn't it, this belief in a God who is not known. On what is this belief based? The world is a vale of tears and we see no God to help us and put an end to all suffering. Is it based on the hope that there is a God and that everything will turn out fine in the end? Is it because of our fear that if there is no God, everything is meaningless? Or is there something else? Does man have an intuition, a primal instinct, a deep longing for a deeper Reality than the visible reality alone? I think that this is the case. If the belief in God were based on hope alone, this belief would have disappeared long ago, considering human history. In all ages, however, there have been people who have 'attained' God and have witnessed to this in their own way.

If we realize that faith in the existence of God is a primal instinct, and that there are always people who confirm the existence of God, surely we can no longer be content with believing in a separate, unattainable God? But what can we do then? We would dearly like to experience unity with God (the second point of view), but why don't we succeed? Is it because, in our era, society is submerged in materialism instead of spirituality? Are there no true Gurus anymore?

It is a fact, however, that through true spiritual practice, the 'breath of infinity'—the Absolute—can rise to our perception from the depth of our soul, in the silence of a peaceful, clear consciousness of Self. If we have an experience like this, at first this seems to be something outside of us, but we are that! It is through the realization that in the depth of our soul we have a connection with that which is eternal, that we become aware of our 'relationship' with God. This awareness means a deep insight into the nature of existence. If THAT is the origin of our being, surely we should live in harmony with 'It' as much as possible! But why don't people do so? Thousands of years ago, the Rishis already said that people do not know 'It', that they are 'ignorant' about the true nature of existence—Reality.

The conclusion on this level (the second point of view) is as follows: man is, in essence, 'Divine' (God-like), but the Divine in man reveals itself only to the extent that man expresses this in his/ her thinking and actions (Dharma). So the Absolute, the origin of all that is, has become man (and all other forms of life), but this Divine origin is only expressed to a limited extent. In other words, there is union of the human soul with the Absolute, but no identification on account of the very limited revelation of the divine qualities in man.

This second point of view, however, was not the final conclusion of the Rishis philosophical search. Meditating and observing, the yogis penetrated deeper into the depths of their own soul. With their attention focused on the 'Self', they understood the Absolute to be immanent as well as transcendent. This means that Reality was perceived as the inner soul (inside, immanent) which at the same time was the outside cosmic soul, the Absolute (outside, transcendent). Inside turned out to be outside and outside turned out to be inside.

This vision is exactly what the Rishis want to express with the holy sound of OM, written in Sanskrit as ॐ . This symbol, the sound of the Absolute, represents the Divine eternal Reality with which the Hindu knows himself to be united in the depth of his soul.

At this level of Self-realization, human thoughts and emotions are seen as transient, and therefore as not real. With the consciousness focused on infinity (OM), the enlightened yogi considers everything that is changeable to be relative and unreal compared to THAT (which he experiences himself to be in essence). This leads to the first point of view mentioned above—total identity of the human soul and the Absolute.

The difference between this and the second point of view is that whatever is seen from the second point of view as being 'not Divine' is considered from the highest level qualified as being 'not real'. From this level of insight, all our thoughts and worries are nothing but obstacles to be overcome on our spiritual journey. At the highest level of insight, we can conclude that the human soul is in essence the same as the Absolute. The relationship between the Absolute and man can therefore be formulated as: the Absolute has become man, man is the Absolute.

Although it is not given to many to be able to 'unravel' this mystery, it is very likely that it happens (how frequently I dare not say) that in the last moments of life (when all ego nonsense is seen to be meaningless) people receive the 'grace' of the liberating insight into Reality, which enables them to depart ('coming Home') in peace.

d) Does the Absolute Have 'Characteristics?'

Now that I've tried to explain the relationship between the Absolute and man, I will next look at the nature of the Absolute as such. Does the Absolute, as 'highest person'—the timeless source of all that lives—have any characteristics, or is 'It' without characteristics?

All living beings have the Absolute as the foundation of their existence. The Absolute is the source of energy that manifests as the human beings that we have become. However, if we experience the Absolute as our highest Self, the Absolute seems to be one and without characteristics; nevertheless, all our actions (preceded by emotions and thoughts) arise fundamentally out of the Absolute. Although we don't know this, all our striving for 'happiness' (in all the various ways in which we interpret this fundamental longing) is a striving for the experience of union with our deepest Self. (For the explanation of why this is so, see Part III, Tantra.)

As mentioned earlier, the more we adapt ourselves to Dharma (see also Part IV), the more we live in harmony with our inner 'Self', the Absolute. In that way too we can say that our characteristics are indirectly those of the Absolute. So, from our point of view, we can say that the characteristics of Dharma (as life should be) match with the essence of the Absolute. Only in that way we can talk about 'characteristics' of the Absolute.

e) Can the Absolute Intervene in Our Lives?

Earlier on I said that God can only intervene in our lives if we allow God into our lives (if we live in harmony with Dharma). This opinion may seem too simple to you. You think that you are living according to Dharma, but you do not see God intervening in your life. Why is this so? To live in harmony with Dharma means a lot more than you should superficially think. The whole of life is a gigantic revelation of the Absolute, a continuous stream of Dharma (natural good). We should be able to see 'It' (the Absolute) in the eyes of a child, a sunset, human compassion, love, spiritual wisdom, the (pure) air that we breathe, etc. In short, the whole life cycle of birth and death, growing up, getting older and everything that happens in this cycle is, as Dharma, an expression of the Divine in the world. It is a gigantic process of spiritual growth through which the Absolute reveals itself in the material (the world). The more we become 'seers' (this means seeing the Absolute as 'cause and purpose' of all the events of our life) the more we see that it is God or the Divine who is present and who offers us countless opportunities to 'adjust ourselves' to life as it is meant to be. In that sense, if we could see 'truth' as it is, we would be able to see how God interferes in our lives. The more we ignore the given opportunities the less we experience the Divine in our life. We can use the following metaphor: the needle of the compass of our lives always points in the direction of the Absolute but in our ignorance we continually end up off course. Sooner or later, this creates suffering and then through reacting to the always present 'course corrections' of God we can find the right direction again.

f) If the Absolute is 'Perfect', Why Then is There So Much Misery in the World?

The answer to this question should be clear now. As said before: man is ignorant about the Reality of his/her existence. This Reality is: the human soul is identical to the cosmic soul, the Absolute. By lack of knowledge about the ego—the 'I' (see Part IV)—we get stuck in the spell of the outside world. Because of this, we direct our life energy, with which we are lavishly provided, to that outside world. By our identification with our thoughts, we put all our energy in the many stimuli that come to us from the outside. It is obvious that the less we are ourselves, the more we react to these stimuli.

Living in the sphere of relativity, the world of duality, man throws all his energy into the daily battle, often with inhuman consequences as a result. And extreme inhumanity so often ends in the madness of a war. From this, you can see how dangerous the mass ignorance about the Reality of life can be.

There have doubtless always been many good, positive people, who have not understood why God allows so much wrong and misery to happen. The answer to all such questions is: all evil results from ignorance (about Reality) and God, that is to say, the Absolute—Reality—can only intervene in the world as far as man lets this happen through himself, in his/her own mind.

2.05 The Illusion of the Visible World

After this extensive attempt to 'speak about the unspeakable' (the Absolute), we will pick up the line of our initiation again. I have explained that when we want to follow the path of Jnana Yoga, we must learn to distinguish between the relative (temporary) and the absolute (timeless) aspects of life. In my view, we have made this distinction clear enough now and one can reflect on this oneself.

Now we must give names to the two aspects between which we have to distinguish. The ancient Hindu sages called the totality of all the relative aspects of life 'Maya'. When we translate this term literally from the Sanskrit, it means 'illusion'. This does not mean that the sages denied the relative reality—that is to say, the world we live in. But by using the word 'illusion', they want to tell us that we will be deceived when we consider the temporally existence to be the only reality.

In mysticism, something is considered to be real only when it cannot be *not* there—meaning, when it is always there, without beginning and without end (unborn, immortal). This can only be said of the Absolute. The goal is to find that Absolute.

One can also define the concept of 'Maya' as 'all that makes us forget our true nature'. (Even though we are a manifestation of the Divine, we are hypnotized by the world and therefore forget our true nature.)

The true meaning of Maya is to give us a much deeper insight into the relativity of things. Actually, it makes little sense to talk about Maya if one does not see that which is not Maya. It is this 'not Maya' (Reality) that the ancient Hindu sages want us to discover.

2.06 To Name the Unnamable

When we use the term 'Reality', we must realize that each definition of this 'great unknown' is a limitation. It is not just 'that which is not limited by time and space'. It is not just 'that which is unborn and immortal'. What 'IT' is cannot be expressed in words. Still, the ancient seers use a term for this unknown. This is for practical reasons, because it is so laborious if you always have to say that everything you can say about it, is not That. When we keep this in mind at any time, then we can introduce a name for this unknown.

That great unknown, the Absolute, which has to be discovered, is on behalf of the philosophical and religious indication determined to be Brahman. In Sanskrit, this word has the meaning of expansion. Probably the ancient Hindus wanted to indicate herewith that Reality is as the limitless 'great void,' in which the universe expands.

2.07 Without Brahman Nothing Can Exist

After this explanation, we can briefly say that relative reality is Maya, and the absolute Reality is Brahman. Maya and Brahman look like two different concepts. It looks as if Maya exists apart from Brahman, and that Brahman has no relationship with Maya. But actually we do not see the connection between Maya and Brahman. Brahman IS, independent of whether there is Maya or not. Maya, however, can only exist because there is Brahman. At first there is Brahman, then the manifestation of all that has appeared in it—Maya.

Therefore: Brahman—Reality—became Maya, the relative reality. Because of this, one can also say: everything is Brahman. That is to say, the relative turns out to be Brahman. Though we use these two concepts to distinguish the relative, temporary, from the Absolute, the timeless, the relationship between them must be clear now. All that came into being, Maya, is a manifestation, an expression of that in which everything came into being, Brahman.

2.08 What is the Connection Between Brahman and Maya?

But, more precisely, how then does this relationship between Maya and Brahman work? Brahman has become all that exists. Existence— what exactly is this? Man is aware that he/she exists. If we look at the level of awareness of all that lives, we can roughly distinguish three levels of awareness: that of man, animals, and plants.

As for human beings, we can distinguish between the consciousness and the sub-consciousness. Animals live in a subconscious state (no awareness of the 'self')—that is to say, past experiences are apparently stored somewhere, considering the animal's 'remembered' reactions of fear or joyful recognition.

Plants' level of awareness, beneath that of animals, cannot be perceived by us, so we can only suppose that it is there.

For this explanation, we will now limit ourselves to the human state of consciousness. From the unconscious state of the little child, different levels of awareness of the self slowly develop. Through puberty and adolescence, man should reach inner maturity. From a spiritual point of view, as seen by the ancient Hindu sages, inner maturity means that one has attained his true Self (the Absolute—Brahman). We can say of such a person that he/she is finished—completed. 'Spirit' has become conscious, manifested in 'matter'.

Brahman is revealed in an enlightened being, who knows he/she is Brahman, and he/she sees Brahman in others too. In the combination of body and mind—that is to say, in Maya—Brahman proves to be present. From this enlightened point of view, there is no doubt that in all that lives, what belongs to the relative—to Maya—is Brahman. Only in man does the possibility for revelation of the Absolute, the realization of Reality, of Brahman, exist. Through this, the connection between Maya and Brahman will be clear. This connection is: consciousness.

As mentioned earlier, in the Bible, this relationship is revealed as: 'God created Man in His Own image.' This image is consciousness, and not the body, of course. And Jesus, the enlightened one himself said, 'The Father and I are one.' That is to say, in essence the same—pure, undivided, timeless, absolute consciousness.

2.09 The Divine in Man

This brings us to the next concept: that in the human being, what is not Maya (temporary), but rather Brahman, is called 'Atman'. Although one can say that Atman is Brahman, the 'Divine' in man, with regard to its creative power, Atman is not equal to Brahman.

Just imagine the immense ocean. You draw a cup of water and examine one drop. The essence of that one drop is equal to the essence of the ocean. But the immense ocean has a tremendous power—which, of course, the drop doesn't have. Still, the composition of the drop is the same as the ocean. Or a fire, for instance; a spark of a big fire has the same composition as that fire, but lacks the power to arouse the intense heat of the big fire.

I think by these examples one can understand that there have been mystics who've said, 'I am God.' This means (in our concepts) that they understood that Atman is (the same as) Brahman. It will be obvious now that mystics who express themselves in this way don't mean to say that they possess the same power as the Absolute. However creative an enlightened mystic can be, as a human being he remains subject to the laws of nature.

2.10 Not Two

Up till now we have introduced and explained three concepts. These are: Brahman, Atman and Maya. Although they are different, they are different aspects of one Reality, Brahman, or the Absolute. If we want to translate this trinity into concepts of our culture, we can say, 'God (Brahman)', 'the Holy Spirit (Atman)', and 'the world (Maya)'.

Now we have come to know these three concepts, we can proceed with possibly the most profound philosophy there is: Advaita Vedanta. The word 'Advaita' literally means, 'not dual'. This means that all that is, in essence is one, not two—not different. As I explained earlier, in the end everything is Brahman, the One. The word 'Vedanta' means: the ultimate (ante) knowledge (Ved).

So, the Advaita Vedanta is about the ultimate knowledge of non-duality (or one-ness) as laid down in the sacred books of the Hindus, the Vedas (dated 3000-4000 years ago).

These old Hindu scriptures contain mystical hymns and rituals. As the Vedas developed, they became more and more philosophical—and, in the end, monotheistic. What was expressed was that everything that exists has ultimately one and the same Divine source (God)—or, in other words, 'Everything that exists originates from One'.

Superficially, this may seem contradictory to the many gods and goddesses in Hinduism, but it is not because the Hindu considers these gods and goddesses as different aspects of one cosmic, divine principle—Brahman. So when we talk about Advaita Vedanta, we talk about the teaching of oneness, as expressed at the end of the Vedas. When we want to study Advaita Vedanta, the deeper meaning of concepts like Maya, Brahman, and Atman, the differences as well as the similarities must really be understood.

Although this may appear to be only 'intellectual work', it gives much more. One starts seeing many things in a different way. Through this knowledge one sees connections and begins to understand things that were not perceived before. Still, in spite of this gained in-depth knowledge, this is not yet insight into Reality, or enlightenment.

The student who now understands what Maya is and who now knows that Atman has the same essence as Brahman, now has as his/her only aim to come to know Atman. So the question for the initiate is, 'How can Atman in its unity with Brahman be uncovered?' I purposely say 'the initiate' because it makes no sense to practice the following meditation technique if you don't know what mystic secret (the secret of unity in all diversity) is going to be revealed. So, the question can also be formulated as, 'How do I discover the divine spark, which is supposed to be in me, which I seem to be myself?'

2.11 Meditation

This brings us to the subject of meditation. First of all we can say that meditation is the most appropriate (natural) way to calm the mind. This inner calmness is necessary because it is our mind—our ego—that prevents the realization of our true nature. In the first chapter I used the metaphor of the clouds that obscure (cloud) the brightness of the sun.

Although there are many meditation 'techniques', I will limit myself to the meditation of the Jnana yogi—which is, in my view, the essence of meditation. As just said, initiation, or a considerable inner maturity, is desired for this meditation. In fact, all other methods of meditation can be considered as ways to prepare for the real (natural) meditation. In the end, if we really discover what meditation means, the state in which we then remain is that of the Jnani, the knower of Reality. I will explain this further.

As mentioned, thoughts need to be controlled. The yogi needs to get 'behind' his thoughts, in a state of conscious inner silence—not in order to come to know his 'other' self (there are not two selves), but to come to know his own, true Self. Instead of directing our attention outward as we always do, automatically and unnoticed, we must turn inward if we want to know our real Self.

As we know now, in Hindu philosophy the true Self is called Atman. So, Atman (as being a spark of Brahman) is in man. It is not hidden somewhere in the body, but it is man him/herself, the essence of man. The yogi who knows this knows that, in essence, he/she is neither the body nor his/her thoughts (ego), but Atman, or Brahman. The meditation of the Jnana yogi, then, is for reason of discovering this true Self, aimed at investigating the self. This means staying in the state of awareness of self.

The most appropriate way of staying 'self-aware' is the inner quest of the 'I'. After 'who am I?' inner concentration on the I-experience follows. This experience of 'I' has to be looked for and held. If you get out of 'I', just calmly re-enter it, so that gradually you become more and more centered in 'I'. If one wants to practice this seriously, one has to meditate at a fixed time and place, on a regular basis.

Seriously, this means that the ego is already so mature that the usual stream of thoughts does not disturb the meditation in such a way that one can hardly speak of meditation.

By repeatedly 'looking inside', insight into the working of the mind is achieved. The yogi becomes his/her own 'witness', and by this he/she will see how sensitive the mind is to stimuli, whether from within or from the outer world. By this witnessing of the mind, there gradually arises a renunciation from that 'thinking mind'.

43

We call this process 'The overcoming of the ego' (as thinking mind). Gradually, thoughts are substituted by awareness of self, not only during the fixed meditation period, but more and more in daily life as well. The substitution of thought by awareness of self is what it's all about. The significance of this is of much more importance than one might expect. The pathway to the inner Self, to the appearance of Brahman, leads through this awareness of self. In this awareness, the answer to the question 'who am I?' can be found.

How can I make this clearer? Well, the meditating Jnana yogi is centered in a quiet observation of 'I', focused in the awareness of self. The inner brightness which occurs in this way can be compared with the inner light of a lantern which windows are screened. The light doesn't shine outward, but only inside, enlightening the lamp-house in such a way that the inner part becomes perfectly clear. Just like in this comparison the true nature of the lantern is known, by continuous self-awareness the true nature of the self is revealed.

This true Self, then, turns out to be: Brahman, the Absolute—that which transcends time and place, that which is always and everywhere. It is that which cannot *not* be there—it is bliss, perfect peace, and it is 'Reality'.

If you follow my entire explanation, hopefully within my words you will recognize the secret, the mystery of mysticism, the omnipresent silence—inside of you and outside of you, as conscious brightness ever-present.

2.12 Insight into the 'One' Shows Us That We All Are the 'One'
If this 'achievement' of the true nature of existence has taken place, the yogi will try to stay focused on Atman as much as possible. This means that he/she will strive to make his/her awareness of Self the natural 'state of being'. If he/she is distracted from this state, as soon as he/she realizes this, he/she turns inside again. This awareness of Self is now revealed as being Atman, equal to Brahman. Of such a man or woman, such a yogi, we can say that he/she always is (with) God. He/she is focused on God, or Reality, as much as possible.

Actually, it is only after we achieve the insight into the Advaita Vedanta teaching that we may use the word 'God'. And still, very carefully, because Atman, Brahman, the Absolute, God, has nothing to do with our personal ideas—our 'it is, it isn't' games, our world of duality. On the contrary, insight into Reality, the realization of the Self, reveals the all-underlying oneness, which surpasses duality.

Advaita Vedanta is, as mentioned, the teaching of oneness. All that exists has, deep down, the same primal cause. It is the insight into this oneness that should be the foundation of true human relationships. A wise man sees this oneness in all people, whether they are brown, black, or white. The One is in all, whether we are rich or poor, handsome or ugly. Just from this we can already see of what great 'practical' importance the Advaita Vedanta could be for the world—if understood on a large scale.

As we now know, it is the ignorance about Reality that is the cause of all human suffering. It is, therefore, of great importance that a mystical tradition such as the Advaita Vedanta of the ancient Hindus is accessible to us, to end our suffering (of being separated from, not being one with, Reality).

2.13 Sri Shankara

The best-known Hindu sage, in connection to Advaita Vedanta, is Sri Shankara. This Rishi (seer) lived from 788 till 820. He explained the principle of Advaita, not two, but one-ness, very extensively. One of his best-known observations is:

All that has been manifested is unreal, Maya. Brahman is the only Reality. Brahman is all that has been manifested.

At first, this doesn't seem to make sense. Everything we perceive is unreal. The whole world, with everything on it, is denied. Then the only thing that is real, Brahman, is not to be seen by us. It looks as if the concepts of real and unreal are reversed. And then, to complete the confusion, Brahman is all that has been manifested. Or, that which is not perceived by us, the only Reality, is all that has been manifested, the unreal—Maya.

Well, now that we are more or less initiated in the principles of Advaita Vedanta, we will be able to understand Sri Shankara. He says:

'Distinguish between Maya and Brahman and, holding on to Brahman, you will realize that Maya is a manifestation, a temporarily expression of Brahman'.

Maya is Brahman as a golden jewel is gold, wooden furniture wood, clay pots clay, etc. Or, in our words, human conscious is cosmic conscious—Brahman. Although our awareness is not clear enough to realize that we are Brahman, man has, as the 'top' of creation, the possibility of total unfolding of conscious, of enlightenment. With enlightenment, Brahman is, as Atman, revealed in matter, the human body.

2.14 Insight into Reality Leads to Dharma, Dharma Leads to Happiness

Looking back over what I have tried to explain and in what context, I see this: the Advaita Vedanta philosophy is the most direct teaching in Jnana Yoga on how to achieve Self-realization. This 'method' goes from deepening the insight into the nature of the visible reality (the continuous change, the necessity of a timeless primal cause) through distinguishing between the relative and the Absolute, and through meditation on the self to knowledge of Reality, also called Self-realization. This search for Self-realization is one's most useful search.

As I explained before, if one has realized Reality, one will automatically adapt to Dharma, the natural spiritual laws of life (see also Part IV). Consequences of this will be the conquest on the ego, understanding and acceptance of life, and therefore, peace of mind—in short, 'happiness'.

2.15 Detachment Yes, indifference No

About the experience of enlightenment itself, not much has been said. The reason for this is that it is not possible to express such an experience in words. Because Reality is present in your soul (Atman), you may become aware of it by my words, but at the same time it is impossible to put this 'taste of Reality' into words. Everything that can be said about Reality can be no more than a 'tin-opening', hoping that this makes you taste its 'satisfying' content. Every description has its opposite. When beauty exists, we know what ugliness is; when we know what young means, we know what is old. And so on. But Brahman is absolutely ONE, self-existent, complete, without opposite.

Words like supreme happiness, pure love and perfect peace are like colors with which we try to color the timeless, omnipresent Reality. To him who knows Reality, Brahman, the importance of this knowledge will be perfectly clear.

The use of the word 'Reality' is of great importance. All temporary things are considered as relative, depending on the timeless, the Absolute, Brahman, which therefore is the only Reality. In the mystical experience, everything is good in the end, and clearly is to be seen that living separated from (not knowing of) Reality is the only real cause of all human misery.

With this in mind, I should explain the important concept of detachment. If you have studied Yoga philosophy before, you may have come across this concept. In Eastern philosophy, it is stated that one of the best ways to overcome human suffering is to be detached from all the things that constantly demand our attention.

The ancient Hindu Rishis also emphasized detachment, but at the same time they perfectly understood how difficult this is for people living in 'Maya'. That is why they taught that spiritual development comes first, followed 'automatically' by detachment. As you know now, the spiritual growth through the path of Jnana goes from observing the nature of the visible reality to distinguishing the relative from the Absolute, and through meditation on the self to contemplating the Self.

This distinguishing between the temporary aspects of life and the timeless 'being' is really a key insight in spiritual development. As far as this insight is developing, understanding of what is really important in life and what less, is unfolding itself.

Maybe you have noticed before that people who have started to live a spiritual (or truly religious) life seem to change after some time. This change will be the result of their insight into what really matters and what does not. To avoid a serious misunderstanding, the detachment we are talking about does not mean that the spiritual aspirant becomes indifferent to daily reality. No, detachment in the true spiritual way means independence and not indifference. Independence means freedom, attachment means bondage.

I hope you do now understand that it is of no use to try to become detached in order to make progress in your spiritual development. This would be an attempt from the ego, which would not work, or if it did, only temporarily. It is better to follow the signs of the ancient Rishis seriously and then, from within, that change will arise.

The adept, the yogi who knows the difference between Maya and Brahman, becomes independent (detached) automatically on his pathway to enlightenment. How can one who knows that he is neither the body nor the mind be the slave of negative tendencies any longer? Detachment arises at each of the Yoga ways. It includes becoming free of the attraction of sensory and worldly affairs.

I think it will also be clear now why this independence is necessary. Without detachment, the 'world hypnosis' cannot be broken, and insight into what surpasses the world is not possible. So please understand that detachment and independence will arise automatically during the process of spiritual growth. This independence is not at all a matter of indifference, such as 'I don't care what happens in the world around me'. On the contrary, when insight in Reality grows and freedom is attained, compassion for the world rises equally, and one feels inclined to adapt to the universal law of Dharma—which means doing good for the world.

2.16 Freedom Means to Be Able to Do What One Should Do

If we use the word freedom in relation to detachment, it is good to realize that freedom in this context has another meaning than it has in our common language. In its political sense, freedom is the opposite of suppression. For most individuals, freedom means the possibility to do what they want to do. In our spiritual context, freedom means to be free from the demands of our ego, as 'shaped' by our conditioning.

For example, a man who wants to have several women may consider himself to be free to do as he likes. In reality, he is bound by his desires and not free to act in harmony with 'Dharma'. Dharma, in this case, means (if one wants to live a worldly life) trying to reach spiritual unity with one's partner. In the end, this will lead to the insight that this unity is to be found in one's own soul (in this way, intimate relationships are meant to bring people to 'one-ness').

Other situations where people are not free to act as they should because they don't understand Dharma are, for example, when they smoke, or abuse alcohol and drugs, as they are an attack on the temple in which the divine spirit dwells.

To put it bluntly, our conditioning is our bondage. Freedom means to be able to do as one should (to live in harmony with Dharma; see also Part IV). That is the detachment, the independence the ancient Hindus were talking about.

2.17 The True Guru

As the Rishis (sages) in the old days had a very keen insight into human nature, they clearly were aware of how difficult it was for people living in the world to become free from their conditioning. As you may understand now, the spiritual path to the secret mystical knowledge has several 'barriers' to overcome. For this reason, from way back, people who had advanced on the spiritual journey offered their help to the sincere seeker. These men and women were called Gurus (see also Part V)—those through which the darkness of ignorance (in Sanskrit: *gu*) is chased away (*ru*).

As Reality is to be found in one's own Self, the true Guru will lead man toward the truth in him/herself. A true Guru will make the seeker independent, living inspired by his/her inner being. The Guru knows that he/she and the seeker are one. It is the seeker who has to discover this.

If this explanation has revealed to you the unity in everything that is, then something has become visible for you of the one and only true Guru—the Guru in your inner Self. It is the Absolute, Reality.

Part III

Growing Toward Insight
Into Reality Through:

Understanding How Creation Works

Experiencing Creation in One's Own Self

3.01 Introduction

Now that we are trying to fathom the ancient hidden wisdom, what kind of search are we doing? Is this religious, philosophical, or spiritual? In the old days, when people tried to understand life, they reasoned, they meditated, and they realized. Their spirits reached their destination. Therefore, I should like to call our search in particular a spiritual one. From our spirit (soul) we feel a need, perhaps a longing, to 'complete' ourselves (although we may not really be aware that we are missing something; see Preface).

When we start our search, depending on our character, we start 'praying or reasoning'. In other words, we become religious or start to philosophize. The mystery of 'Initiation', however, in this context, is that the right knowledge, in combination with its practicing, shapes us into religious people (in the right sense of the word, which is 'reunited men and women'). That is why the 'Initiation' we try to accomplish with this book is based in the first place on the acquisition of the right knowledge.

After we have explained the Advaita Vedanta philosophy, we go on with two other systems of philosophy the old seers developed. Besides fitting our 'Initiation', I think these ancient views will be very helpful in understanding some of our essential inborn tendencies.

Now that we understand that 'everything that exists originates from ONE', the question may occur: how does this creation work? To answer this question we need to study the Samkhya philosophy. After this, we will go into the very important additional question: how do we experience creation in our own Self? For this we have to consult to very old and very profound Tantra philosophy.

3.02 The Samkhya Philosophy—Dualistic or Non-Dualistic?

Now we will look at the philosophy of Samkhya (literally, enumeration). Each philosophical structure is an attempt to explain existence. Advaita Vedanta told us about the origin of existence.

The world of phenomena, Maya, is a manifestation of the Absolute, Brahman. If we think about the question of how this manifestation takes place, we are philosophizing about the functioning of existence. Reality is recognized, but how does the process of manifestation work? This will be analyzed on the basis of the principles of Samkhya.

From the previous texts, we have understood that man in his deepest essence is identical to the Absolute. This is the philosophy of 'non-dualism'—oneness. In general, the philosophy of Samkhya is considered to be 'dualistic' because it distinguishes between matter and spirit (consciousness). Although we respect this common view, we allow ourselves the following reasoning: when one has fully understood and thereby accepted non-dualism, it is not possible to hold to duality anymore, because from the non-dualistic view the Absolute cannot but precede matter.

When we discuss Samkhya now, we will try to explain its concepts as clearly as possible and then leave it to the reader to consider this philosophy as dualistic or non-dualistic.

3.03 In What Way is Life Brought About?

Since everything originates from ONE, Brahman or Reality, the question now is how life, and man in his physical form in particular, comes into existence from the pure spiritual principle, Brahman. Superficially, procreation is clear to us. Male and female unite, and this results in a new life. In the case of a new human being, body and mind develop to maturity—and possibly even to enlightenment (the knowledge of Atman as Brahman). And as we know, Atman, being the 'real I' of man, has always been present in that new human being. 'It' just needs to be recognized. So, Brahman the Absolute is present (immanent) in life and has 'shaped' a body from the elements of nature to manifest itself as a human being on earth. It will be clear that the Absolute, Reality, is present in life from the beginning. At the same time, Reality is transcending life because as the Absolute it is the timeless, eternal, unmovable NOW (that which makes everything to move). Apparently, life is a combination of 'spirit and matter'.

The philosophy of Samkhya explains this combination of spirit and matter in the following way:

> The Absolute, Reality, is a super-consciousness, a tremendous, immeasurable source of spiritual energy. The most subtle expression of this energy, before any material form, is that of spiritual entities.
>
> Although we cannot imagine these spiritual entities, the following simple example should clarify the idea. Imagine a pot of water that is about to come to the boil. The water represents the Absolute. The bubbles on the surface of the water represent the spiritual entities. You could say that the spiritual entities are the first manifestations that arise directly out of Brahman, just as the bubbles on the surface of the water directly arise from bringing the water to the boil. These entities are, however, arising out of Brahman, just as pure and 'transparent' as Brahman itself.
>
> Besides these spiritual entities ('souls,' waiting to be [re-]born?), the universe is full of energy (the 'blind' building material to manifest life and matter). As we reasoned before, that Brahman, being the unborn, unchangeable Reality, must precede everything that can ever appear, we have to conclude that in order to make physical life possible, Brahman manifests spirit (conscious) as well as matter (ranging from subtle to gross). Originating from the same 'source', these spiritual and (subtle) material aspects of Brahman exert a mutual, for life essential, strong attraction on each other. Life is brought about if, in this 'field of attraction', a spiritual entity 'unites' with matter (energy). Then the composition of the chromosomes determines which form is manifested. In this way, matter is 'fertilized' with consciousness—that is to say, there is life.

If we think over these foregoing lines, the following question may arise. As the Absolute is also present in the process of procreation, can we still speak of the transition of a 'spiritual entity' into the female womb (from outside), or is the manifestation of the soul to be born just 'included' in the process of procreation (from inside)? The answer to this mystery may be found if we look at the end of each course of life. At the end, the soul leaves the body, and the body disintegrates in space. There are many people who believe 'that's final—that's the end'. More people, however, believe (intuitively perhaps), that life is a cycle, and spirit and matter will unite again—and experience life again.

This is the common belief in Eastern culture, and the Samkhya philosophy fits perfectly well into this view of life. And since Brahman as 'controller of the cycle of life and death' is both immanent as well as transcendent, it will be by the will of Brahman that this transmigration of the soul takes place. As we ourselves take part in this transmigration process, we will not be able to fathom this mystery intellectually. Close by may come the following summary: the perpetual cycle of life and death is ruled by the immanent as well as transcendent Brahman, just like life needs semen (immanent) to grow as well as 'sun and air' (transcendent).

3.04 Concepts Used in the Samkhya Philosophy

The Samkhya philosophy uses two main concepts for this 'creation of life'. The totality of the spiritual entities is called Purusha ('cosmic Man'). At the same time, the spiritual element in man, the inner soul, is also called Purusha ('Man'). This raises the question about whether we can speak here of Brahman and Atman. On the one hand, as I've said many times, all is Brahman. In the context of the Samkhya philosophy, however, where we distinguish uncountable spiritual entities—which, in the end, became the human beings that we are—it is functional to distinguish Purusha from Brahman. In this way, it will be easier to explain the other, yet further to be discussed concepts of the Samkhya philosophy, such as rebirth and reincarnation.

Concerning the use of the concept of Atman, instead of also calling Purusha 'Atman', we can say that although the concept of Purusha can be considered as being impersonal, like Atman, Purusha is seen rather as the good, perfect soul of man. Here too it is functional to distinguish Purusha from Atman in order to explain said other concepts.

As I said, Brahman divided itself into 'spirit and matter'. In Samkhya philosophy, matter, the energy with which Purusha wants to unite itself, is called Prakriti ('primal matter'). From Prakriti, the twenty-four 'Tattvas', or principles of nature, evolve (I will not go into more detail here). In fact, Prakriti includes all of nature.

If this force of nature manifests itself, and we consider all that has been manifested (the whole visible world) as the only reality, we can say that we are misled by Maya. The external reality is Maya. It is that which seems to be real—which is true, however, only as far as we consider it to be a temporary manifestation of Reality. As we are this manifestation of Reality ourselves, it should be 'desirable' if we should be aware of this.

3.05 Rebirth and Reincarnation

Through the union of Purusha and Prakriti, man is subject to the cycle of birth and death. That is to say, as long as the attraction of Prakriti is not overcome, the human soul, Purusha, is reborn again and again. If at the moment of death all desires have not been overcome, Prakriti still has a hold on the soul, and Purusha will not return into Brahman but will be reincarnated ('made flesh again') through Prakriti—nature, energy. This process of being born and dying again and again, the cycle of existence, is called Samsara.

If liberation—enlightenment—is attained (when the attraction of Prakriti is overcome), and the soul (while living in the body) has again become one with the Absolute—Reality—the soul (Purusha) will not be reborn again but instead will merge in Brahman. This concept of Samsara brings us automatically to such important questions as: 'What happens after death?' and 'Is there life after death?' and so on.

In many (if not all) ancient civilizations, people believed in the immortality of the soul. This belief could vary from worshiping the ancestors to the recognition of reborn relatives or teachers (guru's or saints). In relation to the Samkhya philosophy, the views are clear. The point is, however: can the soul of a deceased, which is caught in Samsara, be considered as having a trace of personality left?

Generally speaking, people believe that this is the case. When one accepts the Samkhya philosophy as well as the common Eastern belief in the evolution of the human soul, one has to conclude that the 'something' which evolves must indeed have a trace of a personal identity.

If we regard the strictly non-dualistic vision of Advaita Vedanta, however, in which ultimately the personality, as being 'non-existent', is denied (see Part II), we should say that 'survival' of something personal is not possible. These apparently conflicting ideas in Hindu philosophy can also be seen in Buddhism, where it is clearly stated that there is no permanent self which remains after death—while at the same time every Buddhist believes in reincarnation.

When the contemporary Hindu sage Sri Ramana Maharshi (1879-1950), who mostly taught through silence, was asked about 'life after death', he said that this question would be clear after attaining Brahman—Reality. When Buddha was questioned about life after death, he is believed to have said something like: 'If I confirm that there is life after death, people will surely misunderstand me. If I deny that there is "something", they will also not understand me. That is why I prefer to keep silent.' This silence has to be understood as referring to Nirvana, Reality, the ultimate state of bliss (see Section 4.16).

Now that we have had the answers of two 'spiritual giants', who are both hinting at the same Reality, we can conclude that Reality is the only thing that always IS, and in this timeless Reality, man appears and disappears again and again, and only the 'ripe' souls merge consciously into the Absolute. And about what possibly happens between disappearing and appearing, we leave it to the reader to form his/her own opinion.

3.06 The Three Gunas

Let us have a closer look at Prakriti. It is energy, the whole of nature. All that has been manifested is subject to the laws of Prakriti—nature. Of course this also applies to our being 'manifested'. Because of our awareness of self, we experience ourselves as being independent beings, separated from others. Because of our ignorance about Reality, Brahman, we do not know that it is Purusha, our spiritual essence, that enlightens our existence, and through which we experience ourselves as 'I'. Truly deep knowledge of our 'I' would reveal Atman or Brahman in us. We have discussed this ignorance in detail in Part I.

So, unenlightened, normal as we are, we go through different stages of development in our lives. If we limit ourselves to the aspect of spiritual development, we can roughly distinguish three stages. The first is the period of indifference to spiritual matters. Our attention is directed only on matter, and any need for experiencing things we could call 'food for the soul' is not felt. As soon as we become aware of the limitations of such a life, however, we begin our search. Matter is unmasked as being relative and fleeting, and we search for values that are more lasting.

What is truth? What is important? This is the second phase. Some people search their whole lives, others find a substitute, an ideal to which they dedicate themselves. Others again stop searching because they came to the conclusion that there is nothing to find. If this is the case, there are two possibilities. Either one falls back into the first phase of indifference, or, if one has a feeling for purity and truth, a certain feeling of happiness and contentment arises gradually out of the acceptance of life as it is.

This contentment will stimulate the purity of such a person as can be seen on different aspects of his or her way of living (food, behavior, interests). This is the third phase of spiritual development. Enlightenment—insight into Reality—is not yet achieved in this phase. The state of liberation, insight, surpasses this. We see these three levels of spiritual development all around us. Most people seem indifferent to inner development. A smaller group, although it seems that this group is growing, is clearly in search of the truth, the meaning of existence. Fortunately, one also sees people who live from an inner peace and who radiate a calmness that is beneficial to the whole environment.

As far as the enlightened ones—the seers—are concerned, the position is a little different. In principle, an enlightened person will not be recognizable to an unenlightened one. On account of his inner freedom, the enlightened one is not predictable in his or her behavior. There are enlightened ones who take on the role of Guru, or teacher. These you can recognize from the attributes and ceremonies associated with an enlightened human being. It becomes trickier when the wearer of outer signs—an orange robe or a pensive look, for example—is not at all enlightened.

When I say that the behavior of an enlightened person is not predictable, I should explain. In Part I of this book I mentioned that one who knows Reality will automatically adapt him or herself to the so-called natural good—to Dharma. In this sense, the enlightened one is indeed predictable, but the point is that natural good is not always in accordance with the norms of society. This means that an enlightened one can behave quite differently to what we would expect. In general, the enlightened one will, out of love or compassion for his/her fellow man, try to bring others to the liberating insight into Reality. It is very likely that he will also take on the role of the Guru, with all that is associated with it. He will do this not for his own sake but for the sake of the student who still sees a difference between himself and the teacher. For the enlightened one, both are the same. The Guru sees Brahman in both, and both in Brahman.

When we now go back to the three phases of spiritual

development, the Samkhya philosophy distinguishes these three characteristics in the nature of man. In fact, these characteristics represent the natural evolutionary process through which the 'gross becomes subtle'. These three phases are called the three Gunas. From the first, the indifferent sleeping state, it is said that man is in Tamas. The Tamas Guna predominates. Of the energetic, seeking human being, it is said that the Rajas Guna predominates. The well-balanced, harmonious, happy human being is said to be Sattvic. He/she is living under the influence of the Sattva Guna. So the three Gunas are Tamas (indifference), Rajas (activity), and Sattva (purity). It is good to remember these. These three distinctions in human nature can be seen all around us.

3.07 A Summary of the Samkhya Philosophy

If we look back at what I have tried to explain with the help of the Samkhya philosophy, it is this: life arises out of the union of the cosmic spiritual principle with matter, nature. This spiritual principle is seen most clearly in man; it is consciousness. The full development of consciousness—that is, unmasking it to be the Absolute, Brahman—is called enlightenment. In the minds of people who have not yet reached insight into Reality (in our day almost all people), three predominant influences are seen: the three Gunas. Man lives under the influence of the Tamas, Rajas, or Sattva Guna.

One can find the Samkhya explanation of the functioning of existence already in texts dated back from 2000 BC. Presumably it was even much earlier than this that the concepts of Purusha, Prakriti, Samsara, and the Gunas were passed down orally from generation to generation. To mention just one person in this connection (just as with Advaita Vedanta we could not omit the name of Sri Shankara), it was the sage Kapila who, around 700 BC, gave this philosophy special significance by his detailed and profound commentary. As you can see, we are not talking about ideas from just yesterday—and please don't think that man today is all that much different from man from long time ago.

3.08 The Importance of the Samkhya Philosophy for Spiritual Seekers

The path to insight into Reality, enlightenment, is often a path with many questions and doubts. The abstract philosophy of Advaita Vedanta will not be easy for everybody to grasp. Its meditation technique will seem impossible because of our incapacity to control the mind. For reasons like these, it is good to know what the sages in the old days laid down in their 'holy scriptures'. In this way we get a better understanding of ourselves and our longings. When the spiritual aspirant recognizes that he is a manifestation of the cosmic principles of Purusha and Prakriti, he will be motivated to overcome materialism and to live a more spiritual life, which will bring him peace of mind and therefore happiness.

Besides understanding how 'it' (creation) works, it could be considered as a 'gift' if one should also be able to consciously experience the process of creation in his own being (Self).

That is why we will now discuss Tantra Yoga.

3.09 Tantra Yoga and Its Place in Our 'Initiation'

By discussing Tantra Yoga, we are going to approach Reality again in a different way. To see the connection with what has been explained before, remember: Advaita Vedanta deals with the origin of existence. We talked about the primal cause, Brahman, and the manifested, Maya. In the Samkhya philosophy, we considered the question of how existence functions. The spiritual principle of Purusha unites with nature, energy, Prakriti. Through Tantra we will try to experience creation in our own Self.

Advaita, Samkhya and Tantra: origin, functioning and experience—three different approaches, which are meant here to complement each other.

3.10 Introduction to Tantra

The ideas of Tantra represent in fact a way of life rather than a philosophy. Since ancient times, this way of life existed in India beside the old Vedic religion. Tantra doesn't take into account any caste or birth distinction, making it popular in the old days—as well as questionable by the caste of the priests.

The aim of Tantra is to internalize our outward directed attention. With this is also meant that man has to face his (external) problems and to conquer them (internally). This 'turning around' of our attention will ultimately lead to liberation, insight into Reality. The word Tantra refers to 'expansion' (*Tan*, Sanskrit) of one's inner experiences in order to become free (*tra*).

3.11 Basis Concepts Used in Tantra

In the entire nature (Prakriti), we can distinguish the masculine principle from the feminine. Of course, firstly and ultimately, they are one. While everything is Brahman, in nature there is a distinction between masculine and feminine, positive and negative, active and passive. The difference between masculine and feminine in nature will be clear to everyone. But Tantra takes this differentiation a step further. On the basis that the creative principle is masculine and the bearing principle feminine, the cosmos is the creating masculine, and the earth being fertilized by the cosmos, life bearing, is feminine— the spiritual principle masculine, the material principle feminine. Together they form the unity of total existence.

In Advaita Vedanta, we saw that the Absolute (Brahman) has become the relative (Maya). That is to say, the Absolute is also present in the relative. From the point of view of Tantra, we can say that the masculine creative principle has become the whole of nature, the feminine. So here too the creative principle, the unchangeable, is present in nature, the changeable.

In Tantra, these two principles are indicated by two concepts. The masculine, creative principle is called Shiva. The feminine, nature, is called Shakti.

Shiva and Shakti together form the unity of the ultimate Reality, the harmony of the Absolute and the relative. By the way, this division into masculine and feminine corresponds with the well-known division in Chinese philosophy, Yang, masculine, and Yin, feminine. Shiva and Shakti are two concepts which can make Reality clear to us from yet another point of view. With the explanation just given, we can say that Shiva has become Shakti and Shiva is present in Shakti. In that sense Shakti is Shiva.

3.12 Shakti as Starting Point

As mentioned earlier, Tantra deals with the experience of Reality as it is. In Tantric terms, this means that man should experience the relationship between Shiva and Shakti in him/herself—that is to say, becoming aware of Shiva or Brahman through experiencing the Shiva-Shakti aspect of existence in his own consciousness.

As we know, the reason why man in general will not experience the 'bliss of Reality' is that his daily consciousness is totally filled with Maya, the worldly reality. The Tantra student, however, who wants to escape from the influence of Maya shall have to attain (realize) his unity with the Absolute, Brahman, through experiencing Shiva-Shakti in himself. As Shiva is unknown, Shakti the feminine, nature, must be his starting point. Because his search concerns an inner experience, he has to start with nature in himself, Shakti.

How do we experience Shakti? Shakti is the energy, the life force that expresses itself as the source of our activities.

3.13 How Do We Experience Shakti?

In Part I, we indicated that energy is in itself a blind, unconscious force. The force works, but man must direct it. In relation to this, it is the blind force of the need to procreate—and the need to stay alive—on which our other, more conscious needs (such as seeking a relationship, looking for safety and comfort, etc.) are based. This primal life force is most easily recognized in the sexual urge. In every healthy living being, this urge for sexuality is present. With animals, the manifestation of this sexual urge is a periodic event according to fixed laws of nature. With man, this is in principle also the case (e.g. women's menstrual cycles), but through the development of consciousness, which is what makes us human beings, the sexual experience can be stored in the mind. This is very important, because this memory of sexual feelings, followed by the identification with these feelings, leads to an unnatural, exaggerated valuing of sexuality. The cause of this erroneous identification is our ignorance about our true nature. This basic misconception has far-reaching consequences. I won't go into this in greater depth here, but I think that you will agree when I say that if we incorrectly value our primary life force, Shakti, as being purely sexual, then this will be the main cause of our dependence on sensual stimuli, of our lack of inner freedom—in short, our subjugation to Maya, the relative reality. The enormous potential of life force that we have at our disposal is therefore not always used in the right way.

3.14 Shakti Needs to Rise in Order to Become One With Shiva

As we have seen, man is Shiva-Shakti, and in principle destined to realize Shiva, the Absolute. We now understand that Shakti, our primal energy, is seated in the lower part of our body, where we believe our sexual energy is situated. Shiva, the pure spiritual principle, is present in our deepest being, in our consciousness, situated in the brain. The fact that man identifies himself with his feelings and emotions means that his focus is more directed to Shakti than to Shiva.

The purpose of our spiritual development from this point of view should therefore be to bring our attention upward until the highest point, absolute consciousness, is reached. At that moment, the reunion of Shiva and Shakti has come about, and we become conscious of Shiva. And this means enlightenment. This is a very well-known concept in Tantra Yoga. When I describe the related concepts, you will probably recognize their meaning immediately.

3.15 The Seven Chakras

Shakti as life force is said to be situated in a center called Chakra, at the very base of the spine. Sometimes it is thought to be even lower down in the place from where the sexual energy in orgasm seems to come, between the anus and the sexual organs. This vital life force is represented symbolically by a curled-up serpent that lies asleep with the head down. This serpent is called Kundalini. As long as this serpent Kundalini sleeps, our spiritual consciousness has not yet been awakened.

Our life force is used through the lower Chakras (sexuality and emotions). We live unconsciously and entirely subject to the natural impulses of Shakti.

There are said to be seven Chakras from the bottom to the top of the body, along which the Kundalini ascends until the last Chakra is opened. At this level, Shiva the Absolute is realized in human consciousness. These Chakras are situated in nerve paths alongside the spine. From the already mentioned lowest one, the others are found at the level of the lower abdomen, the navel, the solar plexus, the throat, forehead (between the eyebrows), and finally at the level of the crown of the head. I will not discuss the Chakras and the development of Kundalini in greater detail in this book. However, I do want to say that there are exercises especially designed to awaken the serpent power, and to send it up through the Chakras. There is a risk of danger if this is done seriously. One can experience an emotional development that can considerably disturb the inner balance. This is because energies are released that the person cannot handle, because the spiritual development is lagging behind the emotional (sensual) development. That is why many Gurus advise us not to practice the 'awakening' of the Kundalini exclusively. The development of Kundalini (if you do want to use this concept of the serpent power) will adjust itself automatically. This is understandable if you consider that if you become more spiritual than emotional (more focused on your inner being than on your emotions, thoughts), your attention will be less directed at the lower senses and will therefore automatically and gradually become clearer. Emotional experiences will then be much easier to control than when you are still living in the relative sphere of constantly changing thoughts.

3.16 Shakti Regarded as Sexual Energy

Every human being knows his or her sexual feelings. But not many of us realize that our sexual energy is in fact Shakti, our vital life force. Tantra aims to teach us how to use this energy for the development of our spirituality.

If I say that man does not correctly understand the life force but experiences it as sexual energy, I do not mean to say that there is something wrong in this. But in order to understand more about ourselves, it is good to realize that what we regard as being our sexuality is much more than that. It is Shakti, nature working in ourselves. As nature has so designed things that procreation occurs anyway, we should, apart from that, be free from attachment to sexuality. The difference between Tantra and other methods of spiritual development is that Tantra does not say that we should abstain in order to develop independence from the sexual urge, but advises us to experience and feel sexuality. This should not be done superficially and incompletely, but completely and very consciously—so consciously that the emotional aspects are transcended and a very conscious inner experience takes place. When sex is experienced on an emotional level, in a mind that is not free, the attachment (possible addiction) to sexuality remains. When the sexual experience is internalized, control and detachment develop automatically. This may surprise you, but it is nevertheless so because the more conscious you experience what happens in yourself, the more you are witnessing your feelings. The more you are 'a witness', the closer you come to your true Self, to Brahman—or, in this context, to Shiva. So by the expansion (tra) of your sexual consciousness in the right way (see also the next paragraph), you will reach liberation (Tan) from bondage to the sexual emotions.

3.17 Not Aiming for an Orgasm Deepens Your Experience

Liberation from the emotional aspect of sex means a shift from concentration on the orgasm, and therefore consuming of vital force to the experience and use of vital force. Why is this so? The energy created during sexual play, which is not released in orgasm, works its way up to (possibly) open the Chakras. When one has already passed this emotional level, this vital force is kept, internalized, and converted into and recognized as spiritual energy. To someone who is experienced in meditation, it can happen that in the 'bliss of the sensual play' the 'face of the Absolute (Shiva)' will lighten the consciousness (experienced as the blissful 'eternal now'). This is the union of Shakti and Shiva (man and God). When one is initiated into the mystical knowledge we are talking about, one will recognize this experience of the Self and then strive for integrating this blissful state of being in his or her life (turning sensuality into spirituality).

3.18 The Use of Tantra in Handling Our Daily Problems

In the introduction to Tantra (3.10), I said that the aim of Tantra is to internalize our outwardly directed attention. Concerning the above explanation of our sexual experience, it will be clear what is meant by that. I also said that Tantra also aims to face our (external) problems and to conquer them (internally). I do hope you will understand now that, in the context of Tantra, this means that by 'witnessing' what is going on in the mind concerning our problems and consciously attempting not to identify with the worrying mind, we will not 'consume'—or waste—Shakti.

On the contrary, saving our life-energy will make us strong, and from the standpoint of being a witness, we will become aware of what is really important in our life. That is to say, the more we are established in awareness of self, the less we are affected by the problems we may have in the outer world. And because of that, with a strong internally focused mind, it will be much easier to face, and therefore overcome, the problems we may encounter in the outer world.

I hope the reader will understand that this Tantric concept of dealing with problems should also be seen in the larger general aim of spirituality, which is finding answers to man's existential quest.

3.19 The Practice of the Sexual Aspect of Tantra in More Detail

In Section 3.17, I indicated how a spiritual aspirant should try to control his or her sensual play in order to gain the power of Shakti, and to profit from 'her' in a spiritual way. Now I will explain the practice of the sexual aspect of Tantra in more detail, especially for those who are not familiar with the underlying aspects of our sexuality (as being an expression of Shakti, our vital life force). By doing so I expect to give the reader a better understanding of life in its fullness, and then in particular in connection with the initiation into the timeless spiritual Reality, which is the aim of this book.

So how do we manage to distinguish our vital life force in our sex life from sexual emotions and transforming it, leading it back to spiritual energy? Nature gives us the first clue. We know that animal procreation is determined by laws of nature. At fixed times, the female goes in heat (estrus), which the male animal senses and gives both the urge to copulate. As far as I know, all animals couple by the jumping of the male at the back of the female. Man, however, is the only creature who can do it differently. Men and women unite facing each other. From this fundamental difference between animals and man we can already see that for us the sexual union is meant to be more than a physical act only. People can look at each other, face to face. This hints to the union of two souls. This aspect of looking at each other, making true contact, is greatly emphasized in Tantra.

This 'soul to soul' contact is only possible when there is love, respect, and understanding for each other. If this is not the case, this can lead to the egoism of the one and the loneliness of the other. This is the well known situation of the man as the seeker of pleasure and the woman often unsatisfied—and, so to speak, the 'compliant object'. Under the right conditions, however, the game of love can be played. This, then, will be the 'divine play of nature', wherein

Shakti seeks her union with Shiva. This applies to both partners; both are Shakti, with Shiva as the inner Self.

As I said, the emphasis in this play should not be on the orgasm. The play is important, wherein the rules of love and respect are essential. The feelings of relaxation and liberation are good. Experience everything consciously, attentively. Whether you are active or passive, you will find yourself in the role of observer, a witness. Observe your feelings. Who are you? Are you the body and the sexual stimuli, or do you have a body with these feelings? This can bring you in an intense experience of... NOW, as if time has stopped. Or even stronger—as if it does not exist at all! That *now*, that timelessness, is very important. In extreme cases in life, in utter joy, and also eye-to-eye with death, the timeless, the eternal, can reveal itself to you. THAT has become the person you are. You are THAT.

I have already discussed the experience of this *now* in a previous part. The *now* is more important than you think. For the mystic, the initiated, everything is enclosed in the *now*. The *now* can be grasped when the consciousness is empty of what has happened or of what will happen. Exactly in between these, in the conscious experience of this, the 'timeless always present' *now* can be found. This is your true Self, the Absolute. To discover the truth of this teaching, as many Gurus will tell you, stay established in the *now*, directed inward, self aware.

3.20 The So-called 'Right-Handed Tantra and Left-Handed Tantra'

It is important to emphasize again that Tantra has to be considered as a way of life that already existed in the ancient Vedic Hindu culture, and that the sexual aspects in it were not considered as the most important ones. The way of life the ancient Hindu sages had in mind relates to the way of dealing with the day-to-day problems of life. Regarding the sexual aspects of Tantra, it will come as no great surprise for the reader to learn that in ancient times too many relationship problems occurred when the sexual aspects of Tantra were practiced. From the origin of life, it is Shakti who manifests herself, which we can experience, for example, as our sexuality. Where animals have no moral problems with this, man has.

I have already explained why sexuality is of such importance to us. Because we identify with our feelings, an enormous attachment arises to sexual emotions. You don't need to read this book or any other to know about the tremendous problems there are in life in connection with sexuality and human relationships (adultery, abuse, jealousy, AIDS, etc.). Because of this, in days gone by, man became frightened for his/her 'inner urge'. It is easy to understand that because of this, the concept of sin was introduced. The sin, however, is not in sexuality as such, but in the ego, which is not capable of controlling the sexual emotions. This made man decide to try to suppress his/her sexual emotions.

The concept of original sin in Christianity tells us in this context that from the very beginning man didn't know how to handle his sexual feelings, as the story of Adam and Eve tells us. It was the serpent that tempted Adam and Eve to taste the forbidden fruit of the tree of knowledge of good and bad. Is this serpent the Kundalini, and does this imply that by purposely arousing sexual feelings, egoism—evil—came into the world? Is that why we have forgotten our true nature to be Brahman, God, the Absolute? This sounds logical. As long as our mind is attached to sexual feelings, we shall be driven by our 'libido', which leads to egoism and consequently to ignoring God.

Anyway, I hope that it will be clear to you now that it is not sexuality that should be considered as the cause of 'sin.' Rather, it is the ego, our selfishness, that is the cause of our troubles (see Part IV). Perhaps it would have been wiser for Christianity to have emphasized egoism as the source of original sin rather than sexuality.

In order to control and to limit the problems caused by the practice of the sexual aspects of Tantra in the old days, the following distinction was made: the sexual aspects of Tantra as explained here (characterized by control and spiritual transformation) were called the right-handed Tantra. However, when people in their practicing of Tantra ignored the norms and values of society, it was called left-handed Tantra. By this distinction, one aimed to preserve the acceptance of the sexual aspects of Tantra by society.

3.21 The Value of the Sexual Aspects of Tantra for the Spiritual Seeker

Tantra shows us that sexuality is a natural event through which we should develop spiritually and it gives us a deeper understanding of the 'flow of existence' of which we are a part. If one is in a position to practice the right-handed Tantra and this should result in an experience of Shiva (who is not different from Reality), one receives the very important understanding of the relationship between sexuality and spirituality.

Or, to bring this part of this book to a close: Reality has become you *(Brahman is Atman)*. This is caused by the union of spirit and nature *(Purusha and Prakriti)*, and this we can experience in the control of our vital force *(Shakti who offers herself to Shiva)*.

Part IV

Becoming Aware of Reality Through Right Action

4.01 Introduction

Now that you have come this far, you may be shocked to have learned that apparently our 'ego' is the source of all the trouble in the world. According to what you have read, we don't understand life, our egoism causes all conflicts and wars, and now we also know that egoism is the cause of our broken intimate relationships. It is time to go deeper into this 'ego' to see if we can get a better understanding on how to deal with it.

In the three previous parts of this book, I introduced Advaita Vedanta, Samkhya, and Tantra—three paths that can lead to enlightenment through specific knowledge. The ancient Hindu sages were of course aware that most people have to live a worldly life and have no possibility or ability to lose themselves in profound spiritual matters. Therefore, they explored for us how we can grow toward insight into Reality in our daily 'struggle for life'. This path to enlightenment is called Karma Yoga. And here the subject exactly is: the ego!

4.02 The Meaning of the Word 'Karma'

Karma is a well-known concept in Eastern philosophy, in Hinduism as well as Buddhism. The syllable 'Kar' (Sanskrit) refers to action, and the syllable 'Ma' refers to cause. So literally, Karma Yoga deals with the cause of our actions. It holds that everything that happens to you in the present has its cause in the past. You harvest today what you have sown in the past. Karma actually refers to the law of cause and effect. All the choices that you have made in your life, all the thoughts you have had, everything that you have done or not done, has finally led you to the situation in which you now find yourself.

Although it is obvious that the law of cause and effect works on the material level of life too, when we talk about the situation we are in, we mean the spiritual level of understanding life. Your material standard of living might be very high, but your spiritual development very low—or you could be enlightened and not have a cent to your name. So Karma Yoga is concerned with how you are as human being.

4.03 Should We Interfere With Our Natural Inner Development?

I do not think it will be hard for you to follow the reasoning that all experiences and thoughts you had in your life have made you the personality you now think you are. It is of course clear that the time and situation in which you were born are factors that influence your experiences, just as personal characteristics and specific physical characteristics can influence your thoughts.

This raises the question of to what extent you are responsible for your inner state. By this I mean, should you simply let yourself be formed by the circumstances of your life, or should you consciously work on your own inner growth, your freedom—and possibly even enlightenment, within your specific situation?

Let's assume that things happen as they happen, and that you automatically mature to the level you can attain. Whether or not you become enlightened, attaining the Absolute in this way depends on the external circumstances of your life combined with your own internal characteristics. Well, let's be realistic. The world in which we live is so thoroughly steeped in ignorance that the chances that you will spontaneously achieve insight into Reality are very small. Maya, apparent reality, has been so emphatically manifested in the world that you can hardly rise above it on your own. It seems evident to me that this is the case; if it weren't, there would be many more enlightened people than there are.

So if one does not consciously work at the attainment of spiritual insight—wisdom—the likely natural course of development, as influenced by the events of life as such, will not be sufficient for self-realization—the purpose of life. This fact is the basis for the existence of Yoga. In the case of Karma Yoga, please let me explain this to you in the next section.

4.04 Where Do Our Motivations for Our Actions Come From?

Following the above-mentioned law of cause and effect, it will be obvious that we should try to let our thoughts and deeds be led as much as possible by that which is right. This seems very simple, and you will probably not see any great depth in this. But beware! What we think and do is not usually determined by what is good or right, but by what we think is right. In general, what we think is right is inspired by our primary instincts—for example, by the need for sex, which can influence our external appearance and our attitude to the other. Or we can be inspired by our need for comfort, luxury, and convenience. But especially we will be inspired by our need for financial benefit. Money enables us to do a lot of nice things, so we all find money very important. Who, after all, is not interested in making a profit?

We can summarize by saying that what we think is right and what determines our thinking and actions is usually based on pure self-interest. This is also why we remain caught in Samsara (see Part III), the cycle of birth and death, caught in the sphere of attraction to the material. To break through this cycle, for the sake of the liberating insight into Reality, for enlightenment through Karma Yoga, it is essential that we stop acting out of self-interest. The point is to let ourselves be led in our thoughts and our actions by that which is right, without being attached to the results of our actions. Whether the results are positive or negative for us is beside the point—the thought or action itself must be right.

So, in order to free ourselves from our bondage to Samsara, the ancient Hindu sages advise us to change the cause (Ma) of our actions (Kar) from self-interest into that which is 'right'.

And because it is not easy to distinguish this right from self-interest, they developed a very profound concept of what is right.

4.05 Dharma: A Key Concept in Spirituality

Right is that which happens in accordance with Dharma. The word 'Dharma' is derived from 'Dhri', which means supporting, sustaining. As 'Ma' refers to cause, we can say that the concept of Dharma is meant to teach us that the cause (motivation) of our actions should be that which supports, sustains life. In Part I, I said that the concept of Dharma teaches us to live in harmony with the spiritual laws of life. It is these spiritual laws of life which sustain life. Therefore, we can also call Dharma 'naturally good'. All that happens according to the true nature of existence is Dharma.

Do not be misled now into thinking that this means that all our inborn tendencies as we understand them normally are in harmony with Dharma. Although we can believe that our deepest natural feelings (tendencies) are in harmony with Dharma, as they come into our awareness in our 'unenlightened' ego, they are not interpreted correctly because of our ignorance.

What does this mean then, living according to the nature of existence? What *is* the nature of existence? As we know now, Brahman is the absolute Reality. When we should live in accordance with the nature of existence, we should live in accordance with Brahman, Reality. But as long as we do not know Brahman, how then shall we know what it means to live in harmony with Brahman? For the sake of simplicity (as Brahman is too abstract for us), we say that living according to Dharma is living in harmony with the laws of nature.

Do we know the laws of nature? Too much or too little food, drink, movement, sleep, etc., is against the laws of nature. This is clear, we feel it. But the laws of nature (Brahman, God) want to teach us much more. To limit ourselves to a few primary examples, there are the (natural) laws of love, and the law of the need for the development of the human spirit. If we can stick to the rules that nature has 'designed' for us, we live according to Dharma.

The natural laws of love are represented in the following relationships: between parents and children (parental love), between people who live together spiritually and physically (partners' love), and between people who make up a community together (love of one's neighbor). To elaborate:

Everyone who has a child knows what parental love is. We can't necessarily take credit for this kind of love, because it's imprinted in us by our creator in order to protect new life. We also see this inborn love or care to a certain extent in most animals.

Love for a partner, on the other hand, leaves more to our own 'interpretation'. The love is in us, but not everyone expresses it in the same way. The less selfish this love is, the purer and more in accordance with Dharma it becomes. Respect for and appreciation of each other keeps a relationship (a natural bond) alive.

To be able to love one's neighbor (which should lead to a harmonious society), we usually need 'regulations' established by authorities we elect. We need such things as social security, homes for the elderly, social services, antidiscrimination laws, etc. Quite apart from that, we can also show in our environment that we value our 'neighbor' as much as we value ourselves. It is our nature (Dharma) that we actually want to do this, but because we have incorrect ideas about the ego (that we are different instead of the same), we do not often practice love of our neighbor.

As another example, I mentioned the need for the development of the human spirit. As a flower needs to open its bud for total self-development, so does man want to become him/herself as much as possible. Not knowing how, man seeks (consciously or unconsciously) in all directions. Dharma is that man adapts him/herself to this law of nature and learns to work consciously at his/her own spiritual development and that of others. In general, this will happen through serving society in accordance with one's talents. This law also teaches us that every human being has the right to development. Educators and politicians should draw their inspiration from this law of Dharma.

Although I only gave two examples of aspects of life which we should consider if we want to live in harmony with 'that which sustains life', I expect the reader to be able to examine for him/herself what is and what is not in harmony with Dharma in his/her life.

The reader might ask, 'Why should one live in accordance with

Dharma?' The examples have already given the answer to this question. As it is a flower's nature to open from a bud into a lovely blossom, so is man meant to open up from the ego into absolute, divine consciousness. The way to liberation (insight into Reality) goes via the road of Dharma, living as much as possible according to the laws that nature (God) has given us. Such a life is in accordance with our true nature (God) and will always 'feel good'.

Living according to Dharma thus means that egoism is gradually overcome and that one chooses that which is naturally good. This leads to inner peace, wisdom—and thereby insight into the 'own' spirit, which can lead to an experience of Atman and the relationship (accordance) with Brahman. This is religion in the true sense of the word, the union, the connection of man with his origin, his creator.

The reason the Rishis developed this concept of Dharma in the past was not to prescribe the law to us, but to advise us how we can become spiritual and thereby happy human beings. The more people live according to Dharma, the more harmonious and 'healthy' society will be.

Then, to end this section, a little something about the development of the concept of Dharma over the ages: When the ancient Hindu wisdom (with all the concepts mentioned here) developed, the concept of Dharma referred in particular to the spiritual laws of life. In a later period ('The Laws of Manu', around 500 BC), this concept became 'mingled' with a social concept of Dharma. Today, this 'social Dharma' is usually understood to support the Hindu caste system.

4.06 If the Nature of Existence (Dharma) is Right, What About Suffering and Death?

Before we discuss how to adapt to 'that which precedes nature', I would like to answer a question readers might have. When the ancient seers suggested that we should live in harmony with the nature of existence, and at the same time describe Reality or Brahman in terms such as joy or perfect bliss, I can imagine that you wonder how suffering and death relate to the good I am talking about. Well, as far as human suffering is concerned, we suffer because of our ignorance of Reality. When one lives in harmony with the Absolute, everything changes, and suffering can be understood as something that can only take place in the ego.

And what about dying? What is death in the light of Self-realization? One who has realized his true nature knows that he is eternity, infinity. For the enlightened one who has reached total union during his lifetime, dying is nothing more than letting go of the body. For the enlightened one who still has some form of ego, dying will mean complete surrender to Reality, the Absolute. The unenlightened but positive one who has become detached during his lifetime could, if he has accepted his death, have a liberating experience of coming home in his last hour, during which the reunion with the Absolute can occur.

In each of these three situations, what is certain is that the physical has been overcome, that the understanding of 'I am not the body' has become very clear.

Based on the fact that in what we call death it is possible to have the liberating insight into Reality, we can also say about dying that it fits into the good nature of existence. The only condition, however, is that one has dropped the incorrect belief that one is the body. On the level of ignorance, of relativity, death remains a misunderstood and meaningless ending.

4.07 It Is Our Ego That Prevents Us from Seeing Reality
This digression was necessary to explain why I dare to call the natural course of existence 'good'. It is human ignorance that maintains the existence of misery and death.

I just told you that in order to live in accordance with Dharma one should live in accordance with Brahman (the Absolute or God). As long as we don't know Brahman, however, we should try to understand the 'spiritual laws which sustain life', as active in our own life.

However, as these laws are very profound and not to be 'grasped' by our ego, which is caught in Samsara, the Rishis (sages) advise us first to solve our 'ego problem,' after which understanding of the spiritual laws of life will occur. So, ignorant about Reality, all relativity and all suffering will continue to exist for as long as the ego is 'hypnotized' by Maya. Therefore, the ego must be understood and 'used properly', which will lead naturally to insight into Dharma. This is better than trying to live according to the rules of the naturally good on the basis of guidelines that you receive from someone else.

With that in mind, we will first look at the question: 'What is the ego?' And that will naturally lead to: 'How do we handle it?' In the understanding and controlling of the ego, we find the essence of Karma Yoga, the way to enlightenment by means of selfless, egoless action. The ego, the 'I', the personality that we think we are, is all we know of ourselves. We may be shocked if the Yoga teachers, the Gurus, say that we must overcome or even destroy it. 'What is left of me when I am no longer 'I'?' Don't worry—there is no reason for concern. The Gurus do not want to rob us of ourselves. On the contrary, they really want us to become ourselves. The point is that our ego should be understood, unmasked as not being our true self, so that in its place a deep, calm, pure consciousness of Self lights up.

4.08 Three Levels of Ego
In order to have a better understanding of the ego, we will distinguish three levels of ego.

Level 1: Ego as Personality
Ego understood as personality, identifying with an idea: I am a policeman, bank clerk, artist, politician, or whore. I am important, totally unimportant, a beautiful man or woman, an ugly one. All of these are identifications with a concept, an idea. None of these ideas is the 'real you'.

This false identification is the first level of ego that has to be overcome. As far as this personality identification is concerned, we have to play the part in life that we have been dealt. But remember—we are the actor. We will play the role as well as possible, but we are not the role. If you escape into your role, you are no longer free. Can you imagine an actor who forgets that he is Johnson and keeps on thinking that he is Napoleon? Obviously we can no longer take him seriously. We meet such rigid egos all too often.

When someone has identified him or herself with a socially negative label, such as whore or criminal, this will be very unpleasant for the person in question. Still, it is easier to give up such identification than one based on an inflated, self-satisfied ego. In a damaged ego, it is easier to hear a voice that says, 'I am not what they think I am'.

To see through this first level of ego—the personality—we do not have to follow a hard inner path. Think deeply about it and you will most probably be able to overcome it.

When we do so, however, we may meet certain deep inner feelings regarding our longing to be loved, appreciated. We want to be 'someone'; we want to be confirmed in our existence by being someone. It is important to understand that such feelings are natural and are in accordance with Dharma. It is in fact this tendency to 'blossom' through which our unique personality can express itself. The meaning of seeing through the ego-level of personality is, however: don't identify yourself with any label (including your problems!), because that is not your true Self.

Level 2: Ego as 'I' experience

So, if we no longer identify with any concept (or problem), we come to the next level of ego, our 'I' awareness. Every person with an intact consciousness experiences himself as 'I'. When the Gurus say that you must overcome the ego (some even say to destroy it), they do not mean this 'I' consciousness. As just explained, in the first place, the idea of being a personality must be punctured so what remains is the 'naked', pure person—that is to say, man without status.

In this 'pure condition', one should then examine oneself. 'What goes on in me? What do I think of, and why? Do I always think when I am awake? What does it actually mean, thinking? What happens when I think?' If you observe yourself in this way, not briefly but seriously, you will begin to see that a continuous stream of thoughts passes through you, as if you are talking to yourself. By observing what happens in you, you should be able to say: 'These thoughts arise in me'. On the one hand, these are my thoughts, but that in which these thoughts arise and disappear, that is 'I'. Then you can say: 'Who or what is the 'I' in which these thoughts arise?' And next: 'Can I really stay clearly conscious, without having thoughts coming and going?' Yes, that is possible if your awareness of self is clear enough. So, if the Gurus say that you must overcome your ego, they mean that you should overcome the thinking 'I'. In other words, instead of always thinking, try to be clearly self-aware, undisturbed by thoughts. The 'I' that remains is empty with thoughts but full of 'I awareness'. This is the hardest thing to do, and it is for this reason that all concentration and meditation techniques are practiced. The 'thinking I' is very stubborn, however, and is continuously 'fed' from the subconscious.

In a moment we will talk about how the 'thinking I', the ego, can be overcome by the path of Karma Yoga. But first a little more about the third level of ego, ego as transcending the 'I' experience.

Level 3: Ego as transcending the 'I' experience

The pure experience of self, the consciousness of self that remains when the 'thinking I' has come to rest, is the true self. Holding on to this clear experience of 'I' means that the attention is not directed outward but inward. As you will remember from Part II of this book, this holding on to this true self is the essence of the meditation technique of the Jnani, the student who wants to realize Reality through concentration and meditation directly on the self.

Although this meditation technique does not belong to Karma Yoga, I will explain its functioning here briefly, because I want you to understand how one can reach the transcending of the 'I' experience and so become aware of the true nature of the ego.

This meditation on the self should be practiced on a regular basis and very carefully, very subtly, without creating too much tension. It should be done playfully, as it were, and definitely not cramped. Ideally, one should sit for it in a relaxed way, at a fixed time every day. In addition to this fixed meditation period, one should return to this pure consciousness of self as often as one's daily activities allow. One should literally 're-mind' oneself again and again. Training this ability will become easier and easier until it becomes a second nature, a fixed habit, a way of being. Our thinking will then be used only in the way it was intended—like a tool with which we can solve certain problems, without identifying ourselves with the tool.

This meditation on one's self, this turning inward, must be continued until this self blossoms and merges into what the self then reveals itself to be—the Absolute, the cosmic Self, Brahman. Then the pure consciousness of Self has transcended, has risen above its own limits and 'received the grace' of merging into the timeless, cosmic, absolute consciousness, Reality. This unification cannot be described any further. This awakening to Reality as it is, means literally experiencing that one is that absolute consciousness. Being enlightened therefore means that one's pure consciousness of Self is 'illuminated' and by the grace of Reality (God), recognized to be the omnipresent consciousness, Brahman (God).

In this context, it is interesting to know that the alchemists of the past used the metaphor of transforming matter into gold. Pure consciousness is equal to eternity, gold. Thus immortality is reached—that is to say, we realize that we are that which is not born, and therefore cannot die, but always 'is'.

I hope that by this explanation of these three levels of ego, it will be clear that when we hear that the ego must be destroyed it in no way means that the 'I-feeling' must be destroyed. Our incorrect idea about ego must be destroyed, the stream of thoughts controlled and the pure 'I' firmly anchored so that there is room for our true Self to reveal itself.

4.09 How to Handle the Ego

Now that we understand that there are different levels of ego, we know that it is the 'thinking I' of the second level of ego that has to be controlled. By overcoming this 'thinking I', which we can also call 'mind', insight in our true nature will develop simultaneously with our understanding of the spiritual laws of life.

Of course the ancient Hindu sages knew that controlling the mind by effort is very difficult. The direct way of the quest for the real Self of the Jnanis is not accessible for everyone. Therefore, the attachment to the world is too strong (Maya keeps us in Samsara).

In order to develop mind control in our daily life, the sages teach us to consciously change our motivation (cause, Ma) for our action (Kar) from 'selfish' into 'in accordance with Dharma', the naturally good.

It is important to understand why right action calms the mind. If the motivation of our action is only to do the right thing, regardless of what this means for ourselves, we become detached from the things our ego wants us to do.

To be able to do this, we should first have some insight into the concept of Dharma. It is a kind of interchange. Ego-less, selfless 'right' action gives insight into Dharma, and this insight into what is right stimulates selfless action. You understand that an inflated ego will be deflated and the conscious self continuously trained. One can also say that the soul is purified. Through the continual overcoming of the small self, the silence of the absolute Self can be perceived more and more clearly. Or, as I am sure you have already heard, you must lose yourself to find your Self.

So, the Karma yogi will train himself in selfless action. Selfless in this context also distinctly means 'without concern for the result of one's action'. The action in itself must be right, regardless of its result (without enjoying the 'fruits' of the action). Even in the beginning, before a clear insight into Dharma arises, it should be possible to make a distinction between special self-interest and that which is simply right.

Everyone can practice Karma Yoga in his or her actual life situation. As I just said, the reason why this overcomes the 'thinking I' is that, with Karma Yoga, action without concern for the results brings about detachment in the yogi. It is namely attachment to all sorts of matters that maintains the 'thinking I'. Our thoughts are with the possessions or favors that we have won or still hope to win. This attachment is nothing other than the attraction of Prakriti on Purusha, as we have discussed in a previous section on Samkhya Yoga. By learning to let go, we become independent. This independence strengthens the spirit. A strong spirit is a concentrated spirit. A concentrated spirit is turned inward.

So how do we practice this Karma Yoga in the daily activities of our struggle for life? A good starting point is the Christian concept of love for one's neighbor, which means acting for the good of another—and especially another who is in need or suffering. Love for your neighbor is Karma Yoga if you do not expect anything in return for your action. Some Yoga teachers hold the belief that it is impossible to act selflessly. Even if the other gives nothing in return, you still benefit from the fact that your independence has grown. So, indirectly, it is to your benefit. Strictly theoretically, this is correct. However, working on yourself in a very positive manner—that is, on yourself as you truly are—is by far to be preferred to exerting yourself for the greater glory of the own ego.

How far must you go in this love for your neighbor, this being ready to help another? If you are also putting your own needs aside for another, do you not run the risk that the other will exploit or abuse you? The Buddha had a good saying for this situation: 'Be as tender as a flower and as firm as a rock'. The meaning is clear: radiate the loveliness, the innocence of a flower, but at the same time be as firm in your right action as a rock; do not budge an inch. In the light of Dharma, this means to approach everyone with tenderness and be compliant. But if you find that what the other wants from you is not in accordance with Dharma, seen from one's own point of view as well as that of the other, do not give an inch and hold to Dharma.

Unselfish practice of love for one's neighbor means overcoming the ego, when you do something for the other, for which you have to put aside your own interests. The 'thinking I' would prefer to stay comfortably at home, and it is a victory over the 'thinking I' when you undertake something according to Dharma. This can mean helping another, or taking part in a positive action, or developing your creativity. You do it only because it is good to do so—Dharma—without being attached to the results. By acting in this way, one clearly experiences from inside that this is good, that this makes you strong, makes you free. When such activities are undertaken for their results, the consequences will be tension and constriction. When action matches Dharma, inner enrichment will always be the result. That is a law of nature. Herein, we can already see an indication that acting according to purity, uprightness, and goodness corresponds to our true nature. It is for this that we came into being.

As I said before, there is an interchange between the effects of ego-less action and consciously acting according to Dharma. They stimulate each other. When the yogi is truly developed inwardly, to the extent that Dharma is completely revealed, then all is Dharma—that is, the Absolute, Reality is seen in all living beings, and all living beings are seen in the Absolute, Reality. All that is good is in harmony with that which creates. Life which is not in harmony, but has become seemingly 'disconnected' from the Absolute, will by definition suffer until the connection is restored. By the way, there are yogis who say that herein we can find the purpose of suffering. It is a natural drive to seek the Absolute, to adapt inwardly to the harmony of eternity.

Someone who has overcome the 'thinking I' and can stay present in the Self, who therefore has insight into Dharma, can actually no longer act against Dharma. It would feel negative and unnatural. There have been many great souls in the course of history who lived consistently according to Dharma. As an example, I did mention already Mother Teresa (see Part I). If you were to translate her Christian background into Yoga concepts, it would not be sufficient to say that she was a Karma yogini. Her religious motivation could be called Bhakti Yoga, but what made her famous was pure Karma Yoga. In Calcutta especially, she took the dying in from the streets to give them love and comfort in the last hours of their life, abandoned by all in terrible circumstances. She said that in every human being, and definitely in those who suffer, we can see Jesus Christ. When you know Reality, living in harmony with Dharma, you can say things like that. Jesus is incarnated Reality par excellence. He who knows Reality knows Jesus. He who truly knows Jesus, in the mystic sense, knows Reality.

From this explication of Karma Yoga, you will understand that Karma Yoga recommends action above non-action. It recommends action in an unselfish spirit, guided as far as possible by what is right. The book from the Hindu culture which treats specifically this right action is the famous Bhagavad Gita.

4.10 The Bhagavad Gita

In the Bhagavad Gita (Song of God), we will clearly find all aspects of the ancient Hindu wisdom. Because it is not possible to reveal the beauty and the mystic depths of the Gita in a few words, I shall limit myself to looking at only a few aspects in connection with the previous text of this book. I will look at Dharma, Karma, Bhakti, and Jnana. If one wants to learn more about this important book, I suggest reading the Bhagavad Gita in its entirety.

The concept of Dharma is probably the main theme of the Gita. Arjuna (man) is encouraged to do what is his 'natural duty'. In the Gita, this is the battle against injustice (adharma). Krishna (God personified) explains that a just battle must be fought. He explains to Arjuna what life is all about. By doing 'what is right' (that which is in accordance with Dharma), man acts in harmony with 'Reality'. The attainment of insight into Reality is what it's all about. This is the highest degree of happiness for a human. It is the realization of unity with God. This is the unity of the Bhakta. It is, however, the same unity that the Jnani experiences, which means that Atman is Brahman (as the drop is the same as the ocean, etc.).

'If it is a question of the right insight,' Arjuna asks, 'why should I do battle and why can I not try to obtain the highest knowledge directly?' In other words, in order to reach the highest goal, must I act in accordance with the will of, and be directed toward, God (the way of the Bhakta), or should I try to attain direct knowledge by concentrating on the abstract, impersonal aspect of Reality (the way of Jnana)? In short, action (Karma) or non-action (meditation): which is the best way?

Isn't this fantastic, a question like this from 2,500 years ago? Is this not the same question we can also ask now? Let us try to understand Krishna's answer. Krishna explains:

> Those who dedicate their actions entirely to Me and keep their attention on Me constantly are very dear to Me and will surely attain Me. But those who meditate on My cosmic (abstract) form will also attain Me. This path is much harder, however, and not suitable for many people.

Krishna puts action above non-action. Action, according to Dharma, to do that which is right, is the way of Karma Yoga, which leads to Bhakti Yoga. It is expressly stated in the Gita that the action referred to is action without attachment to the results, or fruits, of that action. It is attachment to the results of your action that creates new karma and keeps bondage intact. If the result may not be the motive of your action, for what reason then should we act? Again the answer is, 'Dharma. Do what you must do because it is right, and be free of the results'.

How does this work in our lives? Are we not permitted to enjoy achieving something? Of course we are, but you know that the feeling of satisfaction passes, and it is good that it does.

You repeatedly meet new challenges in your life and how do you deal with these? If you let yourself be guided by what is right in the first place, and not by what is easiest for you personally (how you raise your children, how you deal with the emotions of others), then you are actually following Krishna's advice: 'Act according to Dharma and maintain distance from the results of your actions'. This is the way to happiness, which can eventually lead to Moksha (liberation, enlightenment).

In order to answer Arjuna's question more fully ('Which is the best way to reach God—action or meditation?'), Krishna (God) goes into great detail concerning His nature, His being. Thus we find in the Gita references to Krishna as a person, as well as to God in His cosmic, transcendent form. (It is the level of understanding of the student that determines what the true nature of Krishna is understood to be.) Arjuna too (a human being like us) struggles with the question of the true nature of Krishna. Arjuna asks Krishna (in chapter 11 of the Bhagavad Gita):

Now that You have explained to me the highest knowledge concerning Atman, and should You think I am capable of seeing Reality, show Yourself to me as Your Eternal Self (Your true cosmic form).
Krishna replies,
Very well, now you will see everything, but because this is impossible with your normal eyes, I will give you divine eyesight.

Then Krishna showed Arjuna the divinity of the whole creation, and Arjuna was astounded. He saw the Divine (Reality), speaking through countless mouths, seeing with countless eyes, and without beginning, end, or middle. He saw the whole world established in the One, and within the One differentiated into innumerable different kinds. Arjuna bowed before God in deep awe and said,

> You are the imperishable, the Uppermost being, who everyone should know. You are present in all that is created—You, the immortal keeper of the eternal truth (Dharma).

Arjuna realized that, like he himself, anyone else who obtained such an insight into the Reality of existence would be upset and anxious. He saw that everything changes (time) and, confused, asked God for mercy. Then God again assumed His human form and Krishna said,

> I am the time that changes all, yet you need not fear me. Through devotion to Me, man will see Me in My universal form, will truly know Me, and will merge with Me.

From Arjuna's experience and Krishna's explanation, we can conclude that the unexpected experience of the Absolute (Brahman) can provoke a reaction of fear. Krishna (God) reassures us and indicates that this is the 'Divine Form' on which we must learn to trust, and that from this trust the greatest happiness and liberation (from suffering) will arise.

The Gita repeatedly explains how man can come closer to the realization of God through dedication to God. Just as often we are told how we should understand the concept of God. In chapter 13 of the Bhagavad Gita, the distinction is made between the field (the body) and the knower of the field (God). In the field, we 'sow and harvest' (Karma). Krishna says,

> Know me as Atman, as Brahman in this body, as the witness who perceives all experiences. He who sees God as living in each creature, the immortal in the mortal (the body)

will see how it really is. He who has attained this insight is constantly aware of the 'omnipresent' and will therefore not act against the own Atman.

This means no longer hiding God behind his ego and thus attaining the 'highest bliss' by living from Reality.

This answers the question of Arjuna completely. For people who are fully involved in life, the way of action (Karma) is the most suitable. Action in the right way (Dharma) leads to devotion, Bhakti (see also 4.14). The way of Bhakti is the clearest and will lead to the insight into divine Reality. The direct way of Jnana (meditation) is particularly suited to ascetics and yogis.

However, as the path to God is clearly indicated in the Gita and much is explained about the nature of God, we can conclude that in principle it is a matter of one's individual combination of 'devotion and understanding' (Bhakti and Jnana), how to come closer to God. In this way, everyone can use the Bhagavad Gita as a manual for life from his or her own perspective.

The truth of the Bhagavad Gita is timeless. In other words, it is the truth of the timeless, the transcendent, mystical Reality, which is the source of existence. Striving for insight into this Reality is the most meaningful thing a human being (or a society) can do. Why? In his deepest being, man is timelessness (timeless), and the more he/she can live according to his/her true nature, the more he/she will be him/herself—and therefore happier.

4.11 The Purpose of Rituals

We have talked in detail about the actions of a Karma yogi. Anyone who wants to can experience the meaning of unselfish right action in his or her own life. A very different form of action, which can also be called Karma Yoga—an extremely old form—is acting according to a specific ritual. All religions have rituals. The rites of the old Hindu culture are described in the Vedas, religious texts that are thousands of years old. Ceremonies regarding all kinds of events, from 'before birth to after death' and all other important events in between, have been described in great detail in Hindu culture. For their rituals, the Hindus also use so-called mantras. These are sayings and spoken sounds, which have a deep mystical meaning. We all know this sentence from the Bible: 'In the beginning was the Word.' Nowadays, we can barely understand the significance of this sentence. Nevertheless, this saying refers to a very old vision, which was also already known to the Hindus thousands of years ago. This vision was—and is—that one can refer to the mystical Reality by means of sound. To Hindus, Sanskrit is the language with which mystical Reality is expressed in words. Except for rituals, Sanskrit is no longer spoken. Where our language can express emotions or can be used for practical reasons, Sanskrit is in essence a mystical language. Sanskrit mantras and sayings aim to open the spirit to the Absolute. That's why these mantras are of such great importance in performing rituals, and that's why rituals are considered so powerful.

4.12 Rituals Can Lead to the 'True' Sacrifice

If we return for a moment to the meaning of Karma Yoga—action without attachment to the results—it is easy to see that mystic rituals, mantras, and actions such as blessings, etc., were not performed for the sake of the 'thinking I'—the mind—but specifically to conquer the mind. By controlling thought and focusing attention on the sound or action, the mind turns inward and becomes calm, making the vision of Reality possible (inward Atman can be discovered as being Brahman, the omnipresent Reality). It is obvious that from this attitude of giving up the 'thinking I', the idea of sacrifice was born. You give up (sacrifice) your own thought for the sake of what you hope to attain.

We also find the concept of sacrifice in acting for other people's interest. The idea of sacrificing your own interests or your 'thinking I' (ego), forms the basis for a wider understanding of the concept of sacrifice. What we in general think of when we talk about sacrifice ranges from putting some money in the collection plate to sacrificing an animal. I hope it has become clear to you that the most meaningful sacrifice a sincere spiritual seeker can strive to accomplish is the sacrifice of the 'thinking I', the ego, for the sake of that which always is and which has become you!

If you have really understood this sacrifice of the 'thinking I', you will understand that this is also Jnana Yoga—staying focused on the awareness of the inner self. By this, you can see that the different paths in Yoga start to overlap when they come closer to the essential. In the end, all ways lead to 'Initiation into Reality'.

4.13 Right Action Leads to Devotion

There is another important aspect to what happens during the spiritual development on the path of Karma Yoga. In the second stage, as insight into Dharma develops, religious feelings develop simultaneously. These feelings can range from a sense of admiration for all that is good, to a strong emotional search for what is the ultimate source of all that is good. This development is actually a development toward Bhakti Yoga. Karma and Bhakti Yoga, just like the other forms of Yoga, come together. Bhakti Yoga is the path of Yoga through devotion and surrender. What Bhakti is and how it works will be explained in Part V. In relation to Karma Yoga, we can say that it is almost impossible for anyone to practice only Karma Yoga. Why do we take positive, unselfish action for the sake of the good? This good, Dharma, must lead us to the first cause, the Absolute. And who or what is this? If we are able to answer this question by saying 'God', even though we do not yet know exactly what we mean by this, we are practicing Bhakti. It means that we are striving for the good, for the sake of God. We give up our ego, our desires, and our self-interest. We surrender to God. This surrender is very important. Not everyone can achieve this—but if you dare to do so, you will find that it directs your attention inward and gives you peace.

This surrender to God can happen at several levels. If we cannot surrender to something we cannot see, we will surrender to a manifestation of Reality that expresses Divinity for us. This can be a religious statue, a picture of a god or a saint or a living manifestation of the Divine such as a guru, a master or a saint. If we grow in this and integrate the concepts of Karma, Bhakti and Jnana, we will in the end realize that the unnamable, liberating, mystic Reality behind the chosen 'representative' of the Divine, is to be found in our inner Self. In this way we realize the 'cosmic, abstract God.'

It is essential that if we develop feelings of devotion, we understand that behind or in the 'substitute' of the Divine, where we direct our devotion to, the Divine—even if we don't see 'It' yet—must be present 'somewhere'. Although this may seem obvious to the reader now, apparently, for many 'not initiated' people, it is not. Many times, it happens that devotion to images is rejected. People who do so use their 'intellect' for this. They think: the image cannot have anything to do with God. Continuing reasoning like this, people often deny that there exists a God at all.

In relation to this, it is important to understand that for answering the fundamental religious questions the intellect is insufficient (see Part I). It is to be considered as a big tragedy ('catastrophe') that people apparently do not know that religious questions should *not* be answered by 'you just have to believe'. The one thing people should do regarding accepting religion or not is: trying to disclose the knowledge hidden in its scriptures and symbols.

Believing is not enough in our age; what the world needs is *wisdom*.

4.14 Looking Back

When we look back, we now can distinguish the following four phases on the path to enlightenment through right action:

1. Unselfish action with that which is right as only motivation.
2. This develops insight into Dharma. Thinking alone no longer needs to decide what is right. What is in harmony with the laws

of existence and what is against becomes ever clearer.

3. This leads to giving up the ego, the 'thinking I', and the attempt to live directly from the Self.
4. If devotion is added, love and compassion develop, and wisdom (and possibly enlightenment) will be attained.

At this level, all mystic paths come together, and this is where the meaning of such secret sentences as 'The pearl in the oyster; the jewel in the lotus; the mustard seed that is equal to eternity', is going to be revealed. This is where the final mystery is hidden, the mystery that is beyond description.

4.15 The Necessity to Stay in Tune with 'The Source'

Because it will not always be easy to remain motivated to put into practice 'selfless' action, please allow me to give you some advice on how to keep your inspiration alive in your daily life.

It is clear that one who practices Karma Yoga does not withdraw from the world. On the contrary, it is especially in the midst of the world that selfless action is undertaken. The question here is whether it is possible to maintain an attitude of self-sacrifice in our world of commercial and psychological aggression. In general, I think that this is not possible unless certain conditions are met. These conditions come down to this: as long as we didn't acquire the desired wisdom, we must have a 'safe haven' to fall back on. We have to create this safe haven for ourselves in our daily life. By this, I mean that we should arrange our daily activities in such a way that every day we should have at least a half hour strictly for ourselves. During this daily retreat, we will try to tune ourselves in to the 'source'. Depending on what we consider the best way to do this, we could read (only relevant texts, of course), meditate, listen to devotional music, or something else that brings you back to yourself. By doing so every day, we will regain the spiritual energy we have possibly lost during the day. In this half hour, we also can 'evaluate' the negative things that happened to us and try to cope with these things from the perspective of our spiritual life.

In order to 'survive' in a world full of 'ego', therefore, the follower of the Karma way to wisdom has to establish and maintain a balance between being in the world and being 'withdrawn' in the silence that lies behind. Or, in other words, to maintain the balance between action and meditation is of fundamental interest for one who practices Karma Yoga.

This balance is beautifully illustrated by the Hindus in the symbol of Hamsa, the swan. The beautiful swan stately moves over the water. It moves with one leg, the other one is drawn in. The swan symbolizes the true Self, serene above the water. One leg, daily duty, is active and moves to reach the destination. The other leg, pure consciousness, is withdrawn from the water and remains in contact with the source, Reality.

4.16 A Comparison with Buddhism

As you know, the mystic knowledge I am relating here dates back thousands of years. Man has always aimed at a significant and happy life, and the ancient Hindu sages found that the 'gold' of life is to be found in mature spirituality. However, long ago, in the old Hindu civilization, the practice of the caste system started to lapse. Instead of maintaining a natural structure in society in accordance with man's capabilities, people started to define their caste as 'territory'. In particular, the priest caste (the Brahmins) claimed their exclusive rights to perform the religious rituals. One became Brahmin (literally 'knower of Brahman') by birth in the Brahmin caste rather than by realizing Reality by one's own spiritual development. So it happened that there were Brahmins who did not know Brahman (Reality), and that there were sincere spiritual adepts who attained Brahman but who, because they didn't belong to the priest caste, were not allowed to participate in religious worship. Even more troubling, the Brahmin caste often seemed to go astray from Reality and seemed to pay too much attention to the more superficial aspects of worship.

It was in this period of great spiritual 'confusion' that, circa 500 BC, Prince Siddhartha Gautama sought and found his way to enlightenment and became the Buddha. The essence of Buddhism is given in the four 'noble truths' and the 'noble eightfold path'.

The noble truths are:

1. Life is suffering.
2. Suffering has a cause.
3. There is a way to end suffering.
4. The noble eightfold path is the way toward ending suffering.

The noble eightfold path consists of:

1. Right insight
2. Right intention
3. Right speech
4. Right action
5. Right means of sustaining life
6. Right effort
7. Right spirit
8. Right concentration

If a Buddhist accepts the four noble truths and lives according to the eightfold path, he or she can reach 'Nirvana', the ultimate spiritual state of enlightenment. Nirvana literally means 'extinguishing'. When we now compare what we understood from the ancient Hindu wisdom with the essence of Buddhism, we will easily recognize the ancient path of Karma Yoga in Buddhism.

The noble truths of suffering refer to man's ignorance about Reality, which is the cause of all human suffering. By following the noble eightfold path, man's 'thinking I', the ego, is extinguished, and in the remaining inner brightness, Atman is recognized as being Brahman, the Absolute, Reality.

It is significant that in Buddhism the self is denied, while in Hinduism the Self is pointed at as the Absolute. For us, it will be clear now that the denial of self refers to the ego, the mind, and the Self refers to the state beyond the mind, the Absolute (Nirvana).

Asked about Nirvana or other mystical concepts the Buddha kept silent, most probably because he knew very well what confusion would occur when that which cannot be expressed in words is spoken of. If we realize also that in Buddhism main concepts, such as Damma and Kamma are used and that these terms derive from the Sanskrit Dharma and Karma, the resemblance with the original Hindu wisdom will be evident.

4.17 Five Hundred Years Later in Palestine

I don't think the reader will be surprised if we make a little side trip to Palestine now, where Jesus Christ 'descended from Reality' about 2,000 years ago. In Christianity (too), the main cause for human suffering (including death) is a broken relationship with God (the Absolute imagined as a person). This started with the first human beings because they turned away from God, as the story of Adam and Eve tells us. Because of their 'original sin', we all are selfish and incapable of following God's will. Only when we are 'renewed' by God's grace will we be able to live in accordance with the will of God. And to be fit to receive God's grace, we have to 'love our neighbor as ourselves'. So love is the basis for the Christian ethical principles.

When we use our ancient Hindu concepts here, we could say: Entangled in Maya, man acts only selfishly. Because of this incorrect motivation for his actions, man stays bound by his Karma. Understanding the nature of his ego (and with this, the reason for his suffering), he should end his selfish actions and try to live in accordance with Dharma, the will of God. Through this, he will prepare himself to be fit to receive 'God's grace'—*initiation into Reality*.

Part V

Self-Realization Through Love and Devotion Toward...

5.01 Introduction

Now we will talk about the realization of Reality through love and devotion. Although human feelings like love and devotion are 'universal', in the context of this book we will use the concepts of the ancient Hindu sages to explain how man can reach enlightenment through what they called Bhakti Yoga.

Bhakti means devotion, love. Yoga means the realization of unity. Thus, Bhakti Yoga means the realization of unity through love and devotion. The unity I am referring to is the unity of the human soul and the Absolute. I have indicated that accepting the unity between man and the Absolute does not need to be based on a belief in this unity, but I have tried to make it clear that this unity is also totally logical. It cannot be otherwise. Furthermore, the equality of man-Absolute cannot be found on the level of the ego, which we know of within ourselves. It is namely the ego (as the 'thinking I,' mind) that blocks the revelation of this unity.

We discussed the meaning of ego in detail in Part IV. He who has once recognized the unsteadiness of the ego (mind), in comparison with the true Self, knows that the only thing that can be considered to be real is the timeless, the Absolute, Brahman. Worldly reality is a manifestation of the timeless, and as such is also the timeless—but at the same time relative and finite. In the philosophy of Yoga, the only thing that is real is that which cannot not be there. Worldly reality falls outside this, and in that sense is unreal. When man's inner life is entirely disconnected from Reality and he/she is totally absorbed and finally lost in the relative, the time-bound, he/she has missed the chance to understand the real meaning of life.

I also stated that mankind in general lives in ignorance of Reality, and consequently does not see the importance of the realization of Reality. This fact is the main cause of all human misery, because if mankind should know Reality, there should be a permanent ambition to adapt to Dharma. Therefore, the realization of the Absolute is of invaluable importance. The happiness that everyone seeks is found when the spirit is established in Brahman, Reality.

Now we will discuss how this very important liberating insight into Reality can be attained by the method of love and devotion toward... toward who or what?

As long as Reality or the Absolute is not yet known, the spiritual seeker has to direct his or her love and devotion to something or someone that represents or possesses that which is to be realized. The idea is that in merging with the essence of the object of devotion, the true nature of the devotee (Bhakta) will be revealed. This true nature will, at the end, be recognized as being the timeless, eternal Reality.

5.02 In True Devotion, the Aim is Union with the Transcendent Reality

If we think about it, we can find different forms of the expression of devotion. You will find this phenomenon in every religion. In our culture, observable devotion ranges from making a sign of the cross or saying grace before a meal, to a life dedicated to God in a monastery. In other cultures, all kinds of ritual actions addressed to the godhead are performed in temples or other places of worship. In relation to the ancient Hindu wisdom, we have seen (in Part IV) that Karma Yoga develops into Bhakti Yoga. And of course even in what we call 'primitive' cultures, we can clearly observe devotion to 'something higher'; Totem poles, holy trees, and so forth, can serve as objects of devotion.

When I said before (Section 5.01) that the spiritual seeker will direct his or her love and devotion to something or someone that presents or. possesses that which is to be realized, this does not mean that the devotee him/herself is conscious of the ultimate goal of his devotion. In most cases there is an intense longing for a (spiritual) relationship with 'God' or whatever manifestation of Reality is felt as lacking. We now know where this longing comes from. In connection to this, it is important for the devotee to understand that the mystical union he wants to achieve means more than the union with his object of devotion. Ultimately, it means the union of his soul and the transcendent Reality ('God'). We could well ask, whether in all the different expressions of devotion, this understanding of the transcendental aspect of the mystical union is present. Bhakti Yoga therefore makes the following distinction. If this understanding is present, we talk about 'Para Bhakti'—higher Bhakti. If this understanding is not present, we call this 'Apara Bhakti'—lower Bhakti. It is obviously not possible to see from the outside whether someone is devoting himself on the level of Para Bhakti or Apara Bhakti, but it is essential to differentiate between the two. There is no doubt that there is a borderland between Apara Bhakti and Para Bhakti, where the lower turns into the higher. For the sake of this important distinction, I will give a clear example. Religious expressions performed as duties have to be considered as being Apara, lower Bhakti. So if you want to evaluate the religious expressions in the West according to Bhakti, you should consider all prescribed prayers, church visits, commandments and prohibitions as Apara Bhakti. The human mind is very crafty, however. Even if you think that you are performing your religious activities voluntarily, but you do not understand that you have to grow toward the realization of union with the Absolute—with God—we are talking about Apara Bhakti.

What I have said here about Apara Bhakti applies everywhere, also in the East. But in the East there is a greater awareness of the possibility of the realization of oneness with the Absolute.

If I talk about Bhakti from now on, I mean Para Bhakti, the higher level of devotion in which man aims to realize his/her union with the Absolute. As far as Apara Bhakti concerns, this should develop into Para Bhakti. It is a sad thing that in our culture, due to a lack of mystical knowledge, the religious expressions that we could consider to be Apara Bhakti are rather dropped than allowed to develop into a mature religious experience.

5.03 What Is Devotion?
In all stages of our life, we devote ourselves to 'something'. As soon

as we become aware of the outer world (our 'ego' arises), we direct our attention toward that which interests us. Through our devotion to toys, the opposite sex, study and profession, we develop into responsible citizens. This is the way it has to be, but if that is all, it will not be enough to give us the satisfaction of truly understanding life. It is amazing to see that besides these kinds of acceptable forms of devotion, there also exist exaggerated forms of devotion for sports, politics, or any other form of 'idolatry'. Just imagine if man used this energy to discover the 'hidden secret of life' in his/her own self! Apparently man is not aware that this secret is waiting to be discovered.

Whereas devotion in general means praying to the 'chosen one', spiritual devotion in order to realize enlightenment demands much more than that. It means that the genuine devotee must try to establish an inner relationship with the object of his or her devotion.

Although this relationship is in principle one-sided, the devotee should try to direct his or her intimate and personal feelings gradually to the 'chosen ideal' (in Sanskrit, Ishta Devata). In doing so, the devotee surrenders in growing confidence to 'the One'. This surrender can be accompanied by worship (inner or also outwardly). The devotee should be aware that the purpose of surrender to his or her intimate teacher, friend or even lover is to merge into the being of the chosen ideal. If the devotee wishes to consider his or her 'chosen one' to be his or her lover (like Christian nuns do toward Jesus Christ), this relationship has to be a 'perfect one', just like the intimate relationship that couples dream of.

It is the combination of love and surrender which the ancient Hindu sages called Bhakti, devotion.

5.04 Some Thoughts About Love
As love is the bridge to enlightenment for the devotee, it is good to go a bit deeper into this subject. In Section 4.05, I distinguished the concept of love in parental love, partners' love, and love for one's

neighbor. Because the love of the devotee corresponds most with the love between partners, we shall discuss this aspect in particular.

What is meant by this kind of love? The whole day long we are confronted with the use of the word 'love'; for example, when we watch TV, read books, or listen to songs. If we think about the feelings the use of this word is referring to, we can summarize them in general as 'desire'. If you consider how the object of love is mostly represented as beautiful and attractive, it is obvious that desire is associated with love. One needs the other, and this then is called love. This is not the kind of love the devotee should develop for his or her chosen ideal. The only desire a devotee should have is the spiritual desire for unity with the Absolute.

It would be interesting, but also perhaps slightly unpleasant, to test your own love relationship for desire. Please do not think, however, that I consider this desire as a negative thing (one cannot resist Shakti; see 3.12). I just want to distinguish it from the pure, unselfish love that is meant in Bhakti.

The love that the devotee should have for his or her chosen ideal is the love that should be experienced in a perfect spiritual relationship. Not selfish but to be there for the other, just as the other is there for you.

5.05 How to Choose the Subject for Our 'Perfect Spiritual Relationship'

As I've explained, the devotee will surrender him/herself to something or someone in which or in whom he/she believes the Absolute is represented (surrender to the Absolute directly is only possible for those who already know the Absolute). If one feels attracted to a certain image or statue (e.g. of Jesus Christ, the Virgin Mary, Buddha, Krishna, Durga, Shiva, Ganesha, or a saint), and one thinks that the particular image represents all the spiritual characteristics the Divine should have, then that particular image or statue can become the object of love and surrender for the devotee. It is clear that in general a Christian will choose Jesus or Mary for his or her spiritual relationship; a Buddhist, Buddha; and a Hindu, one of the many available gods and goddesses.

For someone who does not follow a spiritual tradition or who feels uncomfortable with the idea of surrendering to an image (although with our understanding of Para Bhakti, this should not be a problem), it will be more difficult to find a symbolic spiritual partner. That is why we see in our western culture that many seekers of truth become followers of a living Guru. The living Guru is seen as the embodiment of the spiritual mystic principle. Surrender to the Guru means opening ourselves to the true nature of the Guru. As the Guru can play a very important role in the life of a devotee, I would like to expand on this a little.

5.06 The Guru: Blessing or Trap?

First, some general remarks concerning 'the Guru'. In the Eastern tradition, the Guru is a teacher who can help a person to advance in his or her spiritual development: preferably to the final goal—enlightenment or the liberating insight into Reality. It is a wonderful thought that one person can help another to grow spiritually. But there is of course also a risk. How can I know that the one who is helping me knows the 'right way' himself and does he or she really want to help me or is this done out of self-interest (money, power)? In other words, how do we recognize a 'true Guru' and what can we, and can we not, expect from him or her?

To make this clear, we will first investigate the concept Guru. As we already said, Guru is made up of two syllables. In Sanskrit, 'Gu' means 'darkness', and 'ru' means 'dispelling'. So, a Guru is someone who dispels the darkness. This of course refers to the darkness of 'not knowing'—ignorance about the spiritual Reality of existence. So, in a strict sense, a true Guru can only be qualified as such if he himself has experienced this spiritual Reality (you cannot really guide anyone spiritually if you do not know the destination to be reached).

Can one recognize such a true Guru? Certainly not from outward appearances. The orange robe, the long beard, or the beautiful words are no guarantee that the person can take on the responsibility of your surrender to him or her for the sake of spiritual growth. On the contrary, with such signs, you should be especially cautious, because it is not a matter of outward appearances. But aren't the outward appearances meant for 'recognition'? What can I expect from someone who looks 'ordinary'? In the Bible, there is a good example that may help us here: 'one knows the tree by its fruits' (and therefore not so much by its branches and leaves). What then are the (sweet) fruits from which we can recognize a true and reliable Guru? Let us look at some of them:

- The Guru does not want to make us dependent on him or her but works for our independence.
- The Guru is not after our money, our emotions or other matters.
- To the Guru, all are equal and his or her compassion is unconditional.
- The teachings of the Guru (spoken or silent) give us energy and bring clarity to our mind and no tiredness or confusion.

I cannot resist the urge to warn the reader against Gurus who do not have the afore mentioned qualities.

The phenomenon of Guru is actually rather complicated. A true Guru knows the mystic secret of life, and he or she also knows how difficult it is for a seeking man to reach enlightenment. The Guru can make him/herself available for the sake of man (these are the well-known, accessible Gurus), but an enlightened person can also decide to lead a withdrawn life, recognized as a teacher by just a few. What both of them have in common, however, is the willingness to guide true seekers toward their own spiritual independence.

A beautiful example of a Guru who did not want to be a Guru was J. Krishnamurti (1895-1986). The core of his teaching was that no one needs a Guru but each of us can find the truth within him- or her-SELF. He devoted his life to giving instructions as to how this truth can be realized. It was sad for him that few people could handle the independence he recommended.

There exists a video of Krishnamurti in which his doctor relates that shortly before his death, the Guru asked the doctor what his anchor in life was. Filled with emotion, the doctor replied, 'It is you!' Krishnamurti died shortly afterward, in my opinion, disappointed in his last moments at such ignorance! The doctor too had apparently not understood that 'anchor' must have referred to the 'Self', or some other spiritual synonym of the Divine. Krishnamurti may have been disappointed that even after so many years of teaching, people can still not live from the Divine in themselves.

The essence of the teaching of the Guru will always be, 'You and I are not different. My being is the Timeless, Atman, Brahman, and that is YOU!' And that is why it is said that he who penetrates into the true being of the Guru becomes one with the Guru and so becomes liberated, enlightened. The mystery of the Guru phenomenon is that there is actually nothing to learn that one does not already know in one's heart, but apparently many are unable to accept this simple truth without some help.

In the proximity of a Guru, one may suddenly experience 'something' in oneself that supersedes normal consciousness. This 'something' can be the beginning of an inner journey of discovery that can lead to the realization, 'In my deepest being I am THAT'— the timeless Reality. The role of the Guru in such an event has been the lighting of the spiritual flame that eventually leads to enlightenment.

But even then, the fact is that 'you' have to do it (to lead a spiritual life). The Guru does no more than give guidance on how to overcome the obstacles on the spiritual path.

If one chooses to consider the Guru as more than a teacher, as the chosen ideal to direct one's love and devotion to, one treads a risky path. It is very important to understand that one has to direct his or her love and devotion to the (assumed) divine aspects of the 'inner being' of the Guru, and absolutely not to his/her human part. As soon as one loses confidence in the spirituality of the Guru, one must end the relationship. So many times people build their lives on a supposed inner bond with their Guru as a person, which causes much misery. It will be the lack of knowledge of mostly inexperienced (Western) 'devotees', which makes many of them dependent on the Guru. This is when the relationship becomes a trap full of risks. If one chooses to be a devotee of a living Guru, it would be wise to develop the same attitude toward the Guru as one should have toward an image as chosen ideal—that is to say, a one-sided inner spiritual relationship aiming to grow to spiritual independence.

In the time of the ancient Hindu sages, the Guru had a key role in the spiritual guidance of people (just as in our society priests could have if they were well-trained spiritually). Even today there are reliable Gurus, but one should always keep in mind that a true devotee lives from his or her own inner bond with the Divine (in what manifestation whatsoever) and does not have to be a 'follower'.

5.07 How is it Possible that Devotion Can Result in Enlightenment?

If the devotee establishes a true spiritual relationship with his or her 'chosen ideal', two tremendously strong inner emotions will be released. First of all: love. Love is probably the only 'thing' in life that increases while it is given away. The more you open your heart to let your love pour out, the more you will feel coming up from inside. Reason: you ARE love. Your deepest inner being is the timeless Absolute which is love and which became you. This Absolute gives, gives and gives... (If It 'takes', this is only to give again.)

The devotee who succeeds in opening his heart for the chosen reflection of the Divine (and consequently most likely for the world around also) will in his/her experience of deep love transcend the level of the 'thinking I,' the ego. The same will happen with the second strong inner emotion—surrender. If the devotee surrenders to the Divine, it means that he or she shares all intimate feelings and thoughts with the chosen ideal. The enormous emotional blockade we usually have (without being aware of it) is taken down. This also widens and raises the consciousness.

When the devotee opens him/herself completely for 'the other', and emotions of love and surrender come free, self-awareness will expand enormously. When this self-awareness transcends the mind of the devotee, the grace of the vision of the Divine, Reality, is possible. If this so happens, the devotee experiences the Divine, and when he or she reflects on this experience seriously (meditates on it), he or she will understand that this Divine is both immanent (inner) and transcendent (beyond). This way, devotion results in enlightenment. From now on, one knows his/her 'true nature', and the devotee strives to establish a relationship with the Absolute directly (here Jnana, knowledge, and Bhakti, devotion come together).

Although the view on devotion given here may seem too hard to put into practice for sober-minded Westerners, it shows us the huge potential we have for giving love and sharing emotions with others. Our usual blocking of 'the being we really are' is the cause of much human frustration and, therefore, suffering. We can also understand from this that, in a perfect love relationship, in which two people are totally devoted to each other in the way I explained, they can reach enlightenment through their relationship. In Hindu culture, the possibility of spiritual development (possibly even up to enlightenment) in a love relationship is seen as Dharma (how it should be) and that is why lovers should stay together till the end.

5.08 Why Do We Experience Peace and Happiness in Our Vision of Reality?

As the path of devotion is probably the most practiced spiritual way (in the East and the West), I would like to explain a bit more about why this path can lead us to inner peace. Devotion is the cultivation of love for the Absolute, usually through something or someone in which or whom the reflection of the Absolute is recognized. Why is this so important for the human being? Why does the human soul find peace and happiness in the Absolute or the reflection of the Absolute?

As we know, the Absolute is the timeless, eternity—that which did not arise but always is. In short, it is Reality. Man is a manifestation of that Reality and, in that sense, is Reality. Man cannot exist apart from Reality. In birth, in life, and in death, it is the Absolute that reveals itself, which maintains existence and which pulls life back into itself. Or, as the Hindus say about these three aspects of life, it is Brahma, it is Vishnu, and it is Shiva. But why is it that man finds peace, happiness, and spiritual satisfaction in the timeless, the eternal?

In normal daily life, man is 'submerged' in Maya, the relative, worldly reality. The mind is full of always changing, non-constant affairs. Man becomes exhausted when, due to lack of spiritual knowledge, mental energy is wasted by constantly reacting to the endless interplay between outer and inner impulses and stimuli. The mind is like a battery that slowly loses its power. Of course, in the human being, one of the functions of sleep is to recharge the spiritual battery by withdrawing the mind from that which changes. But the waking consciousness needs more than that to maintain its inner energy.

The source of spiritual energy is present in the human spirit. This source, Atman, Brahman, Shiva, the Absolute, is Reality in man him/herself, as I indicate again and again in all that I say. It is the unmoving mover. It is that which causes all to move.

Let us continue with the example of the battery. We recharge a battery by connecting it to a charger that replenishes the battery's power (energy). During this process, the battery becomes 'reinvigorated' with the help of a greater source of energy. And that is exactly what happens if we become aware of Reality. By opening us to the spiritual source from which we are living, our spiritual energy is reinvigorated from that source. Everyone can experience that everything that arises in our consciousness from such a source gives us peace and energy. All exertions that are not in accordance with this source tire us, and eventually exhaust us.

I can show you that this is true through a few simple examples. How many times do we experience that, after hard mental effort, we can find relaxation in... nature? By walking in a forest or along the beach, enjoying a beautiful view, or seeking another venue for silence, we recharge our inner battery. This is reaching out, usually unconsciously, toward that inexhaustible source where your own exertions can come to rest and new energy can be obtained (with or without the help of a Guru). If, after mental exertion, relaxation is sought in unnatural things such as aggression, alcohol, drugs, or other activities that we could call a-Dharma, then this relaxation is escapism, artificial, temporary relaxation. But it does not give us renewed inner energy.

It is, in fact, easy to understand that all that is natural relaxes us, because we are (part of) nature. That which nature evokes in us is the less superficial part of us. Should we go even further than experiencing nature and, through meditation (or devotion), become aware of the inner silence, then we are at the very source, the timeless, Atman. The next step is union with that source, which means the realization that 'I am That'. When we have discovered our true nature, we know that we are not Maya, the relative.

Instead of (unconsciously) identifying with his thoughts, man shall try to identify with (contemplate) his true nature from then on. The more he succeeds in this (through meditation or just by being alert or withdrawn) the more he will experience peace, calmness and therefore happiness, because this is his true nature.

5.09 Some General Thoughts About Bhakti, Devotion

I think the importance of 'looking for the Absolute' has become clear enough by now. Through Bhakti, this happens through the cultivation of love for that Absolute. The Absolute can be intuitively recognized in the Guru, which is the motivation for the inner surrender to the true nature of the Guru. We do know that there are different levels of Reality, and that it makes perfect sense to look further than the relative level of worldly reality. As we know now, the roots of our existence are in the timeless, the Absolute, Reality.

Although we may think we do not have a living Guru in our immediate neighborhood, the reflection of the Absolute is present all around us. The only (but not the least) thing we must do is to practice attention, to stay aware. The fact is that all that is manifested is the Absolute, but it is up to us to grow toward this insight. I think you will now understand the saying that 'the enlightened one sees Brahman in all of us and all of us in Brahman'. Behind everyone's eyes, beyond the superficial personality, it is the Absolute that radiates as consciousness. At the same time, all of us are a manifestation in (and of) the omnipresent, timeless, eternal, absolute Brahman.

There is a great deal more to say about the practice of Bhakti in our daily lives. I cannot cover everything, so I will have to just make some suggestions.

Bhakti blossoms in human relationships insofar as they are not based on commercial interests but on true love. Pure love is nothing other than Bhakti. Isn't it wonderful to meet people who radiate pure love? Meeting such people is not tiring. On the contrary, it gives us a lot of energy. Now this will be easy to understand. Love comes from the source of energy, the Absolute. What do small children require to grow up properly? We all know they need love. Without love, development is disturbed. One can say that the love parents have for their children is natural Bhakti. It is not selfish, does not desire *for*, but centers on the desire to *give*. This inborn love is definitely a form of Bhakti. It is the love of the Absolute, possibly aroused by the radiation of love by the innocent children themselves.

As one is usually not aware of this cosmic aspect of love in relation to one's neighbor, we cannot say that this love is a result of our devotion. But it is still good to realize where love comes from and what tremendous significance it has for us as humans to develop it. Maybe this explanation can stimulate you to develop your own feelings of love toward devotion. By this I mean that you can perhaps become aware of the cosmic aspects of your love, and through this grow toward devotion to Reality, which is pure love—in the beginning, in the middle, and also at the end.

5.10 A Saint with an Important Message for Us

I want to end this part with an attempt to draw a picture of the most famous Bhakti saint of the last few centuries—Sri Ramakrishna. He lived from 1836 to 1886 in the vicinity of Calcutta, India.

Here you must not imagine a thoughtful, mysterious, silent and learned Guru. Imagine rather a totally spontaneous, deeply religiously inspired man, innocent as a child, with only one desire: union with the mystical origin of all that lives. This longing manifested itself in a total surrender to the godly mother of all in the form of the goddess Kali. It is characteristic of Kali that she gives birth to life but also takes it back. Ramakrishna longed to anchor his spirit in that which 'brings forth and takes back'—the cosmic principle. That is why he called out her name, and that is why everything he did was dedicated to her. Through his deep mystic longing, Kali came to life in his spirit. In his emotional surrender, he saw her, spoke to her, and lived as a temple priest for many years, exclusively and only for her. He begged her to reveal her true nature to him because he knew that her outer manifestation could, of course, not be the ultimate source of everything. But all that he saw was her form, her outer appearance. He was almost in despair because he had gone as far as he could in his surrender to Kali. Finally, in the urge to pick up a sword and give up his life for this union if necessary, his spirit was totally suffused with Kali, who merged with him, disappeared in him, and all that remained was the indescribable, timeless, omnipresent, and absolute Brahman—eternal bliss. Now Ramakrishna was one with her true nature, and he knew that 'That' had become him. That which is Kali is the ground of all that is manifested. Through this total experience, peace arose in Ramakrishna's mind.

Afterwards, Ramakrishna had two human Gurus. The first was a woman, the nun Brahmani, who taught him Tantra. Through her he learned to see the relationship between Shiva and Shakti in the total cosmic manifestation. He realized that Kali was in fact Shiva, and that his own longing for union with Kali was the longing of Shakti for Shiva.

If you remember my explanation of Tantra in Part III, you may think that the initiation into Tantra by Brahmani took place through a sexual relationship—either between them, or with a third party. This, according to what has been passed down about Ramakrishna, was definitely not the case. On the contrary, it has been said that Ramakrishna never had any sexual contact. He repeatedly said that he considered every woman primarily as mother or sister—and as a manifestation of the cosmic mother of all, Kali. His longing for spiritual union was so great, and his interest in the body so slight, that the limited physical union would not have appealed to him at all. Even his marriage, which came about through his family's effort to bring him back to a more earthly level, did not change this situation.

The second Guru was Tota Puri, an ascetic who had reached union through Advaita Vedanta, Jnana Yoga. Through the path of insight into Brahman and Maya, Ramakrishna tried to come to the Self through meditation. But every time he turned his attention inward Kali appeared, and he did not succeed in releasing his attention from her. Then Tota Puri pressed a shard of glass against his forehead and said, 'Place your consciousness there and never let it go from there.' Finally, Kali disappeared, and the spirit of Ramakrishna dissolved into Brahman. For three days and nights, Ramakrishna remained in this state of Samadhi, as this union with the Absolute is called.

After this initiation, Ramakrishna longed to remain in this state for a much longer time, and after Tota Puri had moved on, he went into complete Samadhi for six consecutive months. It was thanks to a helpful monk that his body did not die during this time. The monk had great difficulty feeding and caring for him. Finally, a serious bout of dysentery brought his consciousness back to the bodily level.

For the rest of his life, Ramakrishna remained in a state called Bhavamukha. He emphatically declared that this was the ideal state for a human being, preferred over total Samadhi because, in the state of Bhavamukha, worldly reality is perceived, but not with a worldly consciousness. It is perceived with an absolute consciousness, in which everything is seen as it truly is.

By the way, when an enlightened person dies, he or she is said to have gone into Maha Samadhi. This means the final big union from which no return is possible.

In this state of realization, this state of Bhavamukha, the slightest religious stimulus was enough to put Ramakrishna back into total Samadhi.

His religious nature made him try out different religious paths; he lived according to the tenets of Islam until, in a vision, he fused with Mohammed and realized the same absolute consciousness; he immersed himself in Christian religious principles and experienced union with Jesus Christ, which obviously again resulted in the same realization of God or Reality.

This brings me to the reason why I have given this short account of Ramakrishna. From his life we can learn that all mystical religious paths, those of the Hindu, the Christian, the Muslim, or any other, lead to the same realization of the Absolute, to the same experience that we can carefully call 'God'. It cannot be otherwise. Our projections will differ, but Reality is one, no matter whom or where you are.

The other lesson we can draw from the life of Sri Ramakrishna is that the sayings he left us from his unbounded mystical vision (as one can find in books about him) can serve as instructions on the path to a way of life more based on Reality. He spoke from his vision on the absolute, mystic Reality.

To conclude, I will try to give a brief summary of the essence of his teaching. Reality is both personal and impersonal. It is impersonal, neutral, like the Absolute, Brahman. Brahman will not become involved in the personal problems that arise out of the 'thinking I'. Reality is personal in the sense that it is the most personal, the most intimate aspect of man. Beyond the ego, in the most intimate self of man, in the 'I am', the true eternal witness is to be found as the Self. In all manifestations of the human spirit that are inspired by this true Self, we can find this personal aspect of Reality. That is what a statue of Mary and child refers to. That is what the Guru, the saint—but also the image of Shiva—represent. That is why Ramakrishna could say that God, Reality, is both personal and impersonal. In the end, this distinction falls away. Personal and impersonal come together in the indivisible, absolute, eternal NOW.

Ramakrishna advised us to turn to Reality, no matter with path we choose. If we let our life pass by without looking for our origin and our destination, for that which we truly are, we are missing the purpose for our existence. When I look at what the world looks like today, at how much senseless violence and other forms of suffering darken the life of man, I can only come to one conclusion: mankind should seriously try to understand life and by that gain insight into Reality, whether it is through Bhakti, Jnana, Jesus, Buddha, Mohammed or any other mystic path. The only way to effect any real change in the world is to come back to Reality.

Epilogue

A. The Catastrophe of 'Not Knowing'

In this book, I have tried to reveal Truth, Reality. I hope that if you have understood my extensive explanation of the different ways to enlightenment, you will be initiated into Reality—or at least have an idea of what Reality means. The importance of 'living from Reality' will be clear to you.

Many times, I have said that the 'not knowing' of Reality is the main cause of human misery. As you now know, this is because man is unaware of his/her true nature and therefore looks upon the perceptible world as the only reality. Not knowing the true Self, man acts from his/her ego (mind) and consequently from self-interest. When self-interest is the criterion for action, conflicts and unfairness will never end. Furthermore, as long as one lives only from the ego, one stays separated from 'That' which is the source of real happiness.

There have always been men and women who have testified to their knowledge of Reality. Sometimes these men or women were considered to be saints. All saints have one thing in common— namely that they know Reality, although they use different terms to describe 'It', depending on their religious background. It is, however, surprising to see that in all periods in time and in all cultures, saints are depicted with a circle, or aureole (from aurum, gold), around their head. It is obvious that artists of the past could not possibly have communicated with each other. Still, the expression of 'eternity' (a circle has no beginning or end), of which the 'holy one' is a knower, is always the same. They have all known Reality.

There have been many saints and many different prophets, but apparently their message has not become common knowledge to the world. The reason for this is that the mystic secret is very difficult to express in words, and therefore to spread. It also happened many times that the mystical liberating insight was not fully understood, and because of that, even abused for 'worldly purposes' ('Holy' wars etc.). This has also been the case with Jesus Christ. This very special saint lived so completely from Reality that he could be called the son of Reality (God). In announcing redemption (coming to God by loving your neighbor as you love your Self), he suffered the direst consequences. He let himself be crucified without withdrawing one word of his testimony. With this tremendous example, he suffered for all of mankind. This means that in our struggling with our relationship to God, confusion arising out of our obscured mind (and what we call 'sin' too) will fall away when we realize that Jesus always held to Reality (God), and thereby conquered all suffering, including even death (because in the reunification with Reality, one experiences being the eternal).

For about 300 years, the early Christians seemed to have lived out of 'knowledge' (Gnosis) of Reality. Then, when Christianity became institutionalized, a more powerful church gradually developed, which based its power on certain dogmas that people were expected to believe. Losing this 'knowledge' and replacing it by 'believing' is probably the greatest 'catastrophe' of human history. Of course, to have faith in Jesus as savior is a requirement for a Christian, but many of the dogmas connected with Christianity are in conflict with logical thinking. These then become a matter of believing. This blocks rational thinking, and it creates never-ending doubt in the mind of the Christian. Anyway, the appeal of believing in dogmas will not stimulate the search for truth within the believer himself.

It is at this point that West and East separated. In the East (Hinduism and Buddhism) religion was seen as a way to enlightenment, an insight into Reality. In our Western culture, religion became more and more a 'belief'. When a religion is based on belief, without sufficient knowledge of its mystical heart, people stay free to do as their ego dictates. There will be no inner urge to adapt to Dharma (the will of God). That is what made evil things possible, such as slavery, fascism (resulting in two world wars), unfair trade with the 'third world'—and, more recently, out-of-control materialism in the US that caused the worldwide financial crisis.

At the basis of this worldly 'evil' lies the global human ignorance about Reality. Almost everyone suffers (without recognizing this) from not feeling his or her oneness with the Absolute (God). The tremendous problems caused by this through the ages have accumulated to an uncontrollable level.

B. How is it that 'Knowing' Will Change the World?

Whether we consider life as 'suffering' or not depends in general on factors such as the phase of life we are in, our health (mental and physical), our relationship with other people (our partner), and our economic situation. When all these conditions are positive, life is good to us. If they are not, our worries begin. This means that our feeling good is dependent on the above-mentioned circumstances. If we get into trouble, we do everything we can to restore the desired balance, and if we don't manage to do it on our own, we often fall back on others for help (doctors, therapists, or social services). However, if we understand that the purpose of life is to grow toward enlightenment—or, even better, if we know Reality—then:

- We can have absolute faith in our relationship with 'the Divine' (Part I)
- We can know that all people are in essence ONE (Part II)
- We can understand the functioning of our life energy and use this to handle our problems to a much greater extent ourselves (Part III)
- We can overcome our ego and do the right thing (Part IV)
- We can live together and be in harmony with Reality (Part V)

It will be clear that the more people who decide to adapt to Reality (God), the better the world will be. Although I strongly hope that many readers of this book will be inspired to lead a more spiritual life from now on, this revealing of Truth would be much more effective if the relevant religious institutions also proclaimed this Truth in an understandable way.

C. The Role of Religion in Spiritual Guidance

No government or political system can persuade people to grow spiritually and act accordingly. This is also a reason why, in the West, church and state are strictly separated. It would never be a good thing to put the profound eternal mystical knowledge in a position of dependency on time-bound political opinions. That is why, in principle, the different world religions should provide their people with inspiration, followed by knowledge. When we look at the worldwide ignorance and the suffering of the greater part of humanity, we can conclude that apparently religion has failed.

Although there are people who think that religion, because of this failure, should be abolished (which will never be possible), it would really be helpful for the world if the different religious institutions and movements were able to display their inner spirituality more openly and in an understandable way. Even if this spirituality seems to have been lost in shameful historic events—or perhaps seems hidden by frightening dogmas—the hidden mystic gold is present inside and needs to be revealed in these dark days.

Although I am aware that it is unrealistic to expect that any suggestions I make here will be followed by the 'spiritually responsible class', I will nevertheless make an attempt for the sincere reader to indicate how the world religions could make their 'inner treasures' more accessible to the people of our time. It would be a miracle if the message of this book should ever get through to, and be followed by, the responsible spiritual leaders of the world.

D. Christianity: Understanding and Practicing the Essence and Putting Dogma into Perspective Will Help

Statistically, Christianity has the largest following in the world. However, it must be observed that the greater part of this following does not put the essence of their religion into practice. Of course we know now why this is so—that is what this whole book is about. In order to be motivated to live like a Christian, one has to have the right understanding of the essence of Christianity.

Briefly spoken, the essence of Christianity can be summarized in the saying: 'Love thy neighbor as thyself.' In my view, the meaning of this important statement is not clearly understood. As long as we identify ourselves with our ego (as almost everybody does), our 'love' for others will be mainly selfish. When we approach our fellow men with a selfish attitude, our own interest comes first. This is what we see all over the world and that is why inequality and poverty continue to exist. So, before we begin to 'love our neighbor as ourselves', we first have to understand ourselves. As you may have noticed, this entire book deals with the eternal question: 'Who are we?' The answer may now be clear to the reader. The Absolute (Reality) has become us, we are the Absolute. Or, in Christian terms, at the bottom of our soul we are united with God.

To become aware of this inner union, we need Jesus Christ as an intermediary. The more we understand Jesus, the more we understand 'The Father and the Holy Ghost', because in essence these three are one—the Holy Trinity. I think you will understand now that, in my opinion, the Christian spiritual leaders should emphasize 'loudly and clearly' that in order to find real happiness and to be able to put into practice the Gospel of Jesus Christ, man should give up his 'boundless' selfishness and try to establish an intimate relationship with the living (timeless) Jesus in his/her own soul. Then he/she will come to know his/her real Self, and after that the love for one's neighbor will follow automatically (Parts IV and V of this book).

It should be explained that any advice, as such, is not meant to oppress or to manipulate people, but only to guide them toward inner freedom and therefore happiness. It will also be obvious that institutions, movements, or individuals that give spiritual guidance must do their utmost to be an example of the Truth they are representing.

Now we will look briefly at the Christian dogmas. From the beginning of Christianity till not too long ago, religion was spread mostly by word of mouth. It took many centuries before common people could read, and even longer before they were stimulated to read and study religious scriptures. To guarantee the continuity of this oral spread of religion, it was necessary to frame the content of the message in a number of clear and attractive statements.

Even today, the Catholic Church lays down the Catholic doctrines one is expected to believe, in so-called 'encyclicals'. No doubt there are many learned people who held that to be considered a Christian one has to accept such dogmas and encyclicals. In the past, when people were not supposed (or even allowed) to think about religious doctrines themselves, this point of view protected the religious system against 'heretics', or even possible collapse. In our days, however, when everybody is supposed to have an opinion about everything, the forced holding to dogmas turns out to have a negative effect on the Christian religion. The growing number of empty churches speaks for itself. Nevertheless, people keep their religious feelings, even if they are often disappointed in the church and confused by the conflict between their heart and their intellect (which cannot accept the dogmas).

So, besides thinking that religious leaders should be able to promote the essence of the message of Jesus Christ with more wisdom, I also think that the 'absolute truth' (infallibility) of the dogmas should be questioned and put into historic perspective. To give a few examples:

1. Will the message of Jesus be any less important if we only metaphorically think of Him as the Son of God?
2. Can His Resurrection also be interpreted as His reunion with the eternal Truth (Reality)?
3. If the virginity of Mother Mary is no longer considered to be essential, will this affect Her holiness and that of Her Son?
4. Wouldn't it be a great relief for millions of people if the concept

of original sin could be explained as a warning to keep the (inborn) reproductive urge under control?

I leave it to the reader to answer these and similar questions. I apologize if my interpretations of Christianity are considered offensive by some readers, and I would like to assure these readers that my only intention is to make certain views more understandable. It is not my intention to hurt anyone's feelings.

E. Islam: Surrender to God, Yes, But Please Let Me Do This in My Own Way

More than any other religion, Islam is based on 'belief'. Muslims are expected to believe that:

1. Allah is the only One to worship.
2. Man cannot know anything of God and that is why the Prophets (heavenly teachers) came to earth to convert humanity and to lead man toward God.
3. The Koran is the holy book for all humanity.
4. Angels of different kinds exist and they are the servants of God.
5. On judgment day, man will be judged by God and, depending on the balance of his good and bad deeds, sent to heaven or hell.
6. Although everything that happens in our life is predestined by God, it is man's duty to ward off evil as much as possible.

Unlike in the West, most Muslims think that religion and state should not be separated (the political aspect of Islam). Islam is very clear in its opinion that Islam is the one and only right religion. Any trace of philosophical reasoning, or trying to understand life in its complexity is not to be found and is probably considered to be a 'desecration'. Just surrender to the will of God and don't ask difficult questions!

When the reader compares the concepts discussed in this book with the Islamic concepts of religion, a huge gap appears. Probably the intrinsic mystical part of Islam (Sufism) will show more similarities, but we cannot look at this here in any great depth.

Unlike Christianity, Islam does not have an ordained clergy, or a hierarchy of bishops, cardinals, and a Pope, as Catholics do. It has Imams—religious leaders who are not necessarily trained or consecrated—who lead the religious services and can be approached for guidance. So if Islam were to develop (there are also moderate influences), then this would probably happen through the Imams. In the context of this book, the following suggestions could be made to them. If there is only one God who created all, then we all are His children (whatever background we may have). Whereas we all have to grow toward maturity (approaching Him), please respect every man and woman's right to associate with God in his or her own way. Don't judge people by their outer religious performance; we all are linked to God inside us. Free Islam from the 'straightjacket' of fear and feelings of guilt (in relation to the hereafter), and accept peoples' right to think for themselves. A tolerant Islam fits better into our modern world and will, in the long term, be more supporting for its followers.

F. Hinduism: Clear Up the Confusion about All the Gods and Goddesses

The several ways to enlightenment, as presented in this book, are based on the ancient Hindu wisdom. This wisdom dates from long before Christianity and Islam were founded. According to an old legend, the Hindus (then Aryans) were given their wisdom some 100,000 years ago by people from the lost civilization of Lemuria (and later Atlantis), who themselves descended on earth from heaven (the universe?). This knowledge was meant to be a guideline on how to become real human beings.

Whether one wants to believe in such a legend or not, the fact is that Hinduism is the oldest of the world's religions still practiced. One of the reasons why this became possible seems to be the strong combination of profound wisdom and acceptance of the fact that each individual has to follow his or her own spiritual path. The end of each spiritual journey will always be reunion with Reality—God becoming known in His creation.

It is remarkable that in the West, Hinduism has never been paid much attention, apart from the increasing interest in Yoga and Indian philosophy. Probably the main reason for this lack of interest is the fact that the known monotheistic religions consider Hinduism as a more primitive religion because of its belief in gods and goddesses. Another reason might be the Indian caste system which, in the eyes of Westerners, shows that Hinduism supports the idea of the inequality of people.

In Hinduism, too, there exists no hierarchy, no coordinating authority that declares what the followers are supposed to believe. Among Hindus, however, there exist various levels of 'initiates' (e.g. Pundit, Swami, Acharya, Avatar, Rishi). We may expect that all teachers on these different levels are very well aware that the ONE they are supposed to represent became the whole of creation.

In the early days of Hinduism, no images of the ONE were made. People were supposed to grow toward enlightenment (knowing Reality) through reasoning, meditating, and doing the right thing (Parts I to IV). Gradually, there arose the need to shape an image, which gave the owner of that image a strong association with the elusive, omnipresent, timeless Absolute.

Thanks to archaeological findings, we know that the image of Shiva (a male figure sitting with crossed legs) is probably the first type of image made by man to help focus on the Absolute Reality. His sitting in meditation posture is significant, because it expresses an 'unmovable, conscious presence' (Reality).

It is not so strange that through the ages this need to shape images in order to come closer to the experience of Reality developed. But the confusion starts when people are no longer aware that the image is not God, but only an invented 'form of the formless'.

The image cult developed largely in Hinduism, and we can

understand this to the extent that the Absolute is creating (Brahma), sustaining (Vishnu), pulling us back from life (Shiva), subject of our devotion (Krishna), giving us knowledge and wisdom (Ganesha), bestowing the energy with which we can overcome our problems (Durga), and so forth.

When we try to understand how Hinduism is practiced today, we wonder how to assess all the devotion we see. Is it really devotion, which is meant to reveal the Absolute to the devotee, or is the subject of devotion already to such an extent personalized that 'transcendental wisdom' is not to be expected anymore (Part V)? Although we cannot really answer this question, we suppose, considering the scale on which people beg to their deities for personal favors, that the knowledge of the pure non-dualistic Hinduism has moved to the background in Hinduism. It is, however, remarkable that people in the West who have lost interest in their own religion often feel strongly attracted to the Hindu view of non-duality.

In the context of this attempt to analyze how Hinduism could contribute to a more 'spiritual humanity', it will be clear that its inner treasures in particular can serve this purpose. On the one hand, it would be of great value if Hindu teachers emphasized the monotheistic aspect of Hinduism much more strongly. On the other hand, Westerners are strongly advised to investigate deeply the essence of Hinduism, and to enrich modern society with its illuminating views—which is the main aim of this book.

To conclude this brief look at Hinduism, some words about the caste system: In all societies in the world, we see people with different skills. This is the way it should be, because we need plumbers as well as doctors, politicians as well as laborers, etc. Though people are different in this way, they are all created—and loved—by the ONE, and as such are all absolutely equal. It would be going much too far here to try to analyze why this distinction into different levels of society ran off the rails so dramatically in India. No doubt it has something to do with not understanding the ego (which can lead to the need to exercise power over our fellow man), and the abuse of the concept of Karma ('It is because of the mistakes you made in your previous life that you are in such a bad position now').

Although officially the caste system in India has been abolished, in practice it still exists, which prevents millions of people from developing according to their talents. Here too the Hindu teachers should 'spread the message' of the equal birth of all people and emphasize that it would be better to value people on their way of being instead of on their caste.

G. Buddhism: Please Reveal to Us What's Behind the Smile of the Buddha!

In Part IV, I explained how Buddhism originated from Hinduism. When the Buddha—the 'enlightened one'—found Nirvana (Reality) through his own efforts, he realized that it was no use trying to describe this state of Nirvana to others. He clearly explained and set out the way to illumination, and described Nirvana simply as a state of 'extinguishing'. The reader of this book will understand by now that this extinguishing refers to the conquest of the ego—the thinking mind—in favor of a state of clear consciousness.

Because of Buddha's decision not to try to describe the indescribable (God, life after death, etc.), in Buddhism, 'the way' is much more emphasized than 'the goal'. The way can be shown; the goal can't.

Although there are different movements in Buddhism (e.g. Theravada, Mahayana, and Zen), none of them have 'prophets' who tells us what God wants us to do or to believe. Even stronger, the whole concept of a God who rules everything from above is not found. All this is the consequence of Buddha's decision not to speak about THAT which cannot be put into words.

In Buddhism, there is no God, but it is still a religion and a very profound one too! Just as in Hinduism, the followers have to go their own way on the spiritual path, guided, however, by the spiritual instructions (how to live to attain happiness, Nirvana) as laid down in the Buddha Dhamma (Dharma).

In Buddhism, the end of the spiritual path is symbolized by the Buddha sitting in meditation posture with a heavenly and mysterious smile on his face. We—the reader and I—know that this 'transcendental smile' must be the expression of the experience of the blissful Absolute, Reality.

If we think about how Buddhism could contribute to a better understanding of spirituality by the world in general, we feel that we should humbly ask the Buddha to reveal what is behind his promising smile.

Probably he—that is to say, his representatives—will remain silent. We know, however, that in Buddhism the doctrine of 'emptiness', or the void, is considered as the ultimate mystical essence. Wouldn't it be possible to express a bit more, in common language, whereto the 'path of purification' is leading, and why? We always see great emphasis in Buddhism on right conduct, but its connection with wisdom, in my opinion, is not clearly shown. In other words, is it not possible to express more clearly that spiritual growth in Buddhism develops roughly along the following lines: understanding what is right (Dharma) leads to acting right (Karma), while the wisdom so acquired leads to devotion (Puja or Bhakti) to the 'great unknown' in the form of the Buddha, with the realization of Nirvana (Reality) as final destination?

Hopefully, this will help people to understand that qualities like wisdom and respect are just (indispensable) treads on the spiritual path and that one has to 'climb' higher in order to approach (and possibly reach) the happiness behind the smile of the Buddha.

H. Manur Bhava!

In this book, I first made an attempt to describe the indescribable. Then I looked at different ways toward enlightenment. Although I used the concepts of the ancient Hindu wisdom for this, I hope the reader can agree with me that these concepts apply to all of us. This demonstrates the universal character of these basic concepts.

Because it is my deepest conviction that the import of these concepts strongly corresponds to the essence of religion in general, and because I think that the different religions as we know them now have gone too far astray from their essence, I have made some suggestions for each of the four great world religions on how they can contribute to a better world. This *is* the task of religion. When religions fail to do so, people get confused, and any disaster you can imagine can happen.

In relation to this, it is very alarming to see how the worldwide credit crunch expanded and resulted in a worldwide recession. Besides this, there are other, probably even more serious threats for humanity, like the climate change and energy crisis. I don't know whether the reader dares to recognize these threats as a result of our straying too far from Reality for what has been a very long time.

All the 'signs', however, are there.

Humanity must try to overcome materialism and learn to live in harmony with Reality. Therefore, let us still accept the advice of the old sages of Lemuria given to the Aryans: *Become human, MANUR BHAVA!*

BOOKS

O is a symbol of the world, of oneness and unity. In different cultures it also means the "eye," symbolizing knowledge and insight. We aim to publish books that are accessible, constructive and that challenge accepted opinion, both that of academia and the "moral majority."

Our books are available in all good English language bookstores worldwide. If you don't see the book on the shelves ask the bookstore to order it for you, quoting the ISBN number and title. Alternatively you can order online (all major online retail sites carry our titles) or contact the distributor in the relevant country, listed on the copyright page.

See our website www.o-books.net for a full list of over 500 titles, growing by 100 a year.

And tune in to myspiritradio.com for our book review radio show, hosted by June-Elleni Laine, where you can listen to the authors discussing their books.

mySpiritRadio